PREFACE

1. Scope

This publication provides fundamental principles and guidance for public affairs support to joint operations. It also addresses public affairs operations and the role of public affairs in strategic communication.

2. Purpose

This publication has been prepared under the direction of the Chairman of the Joint Chiefs of Staff. It sets forth joint doctrine to govern the activities and performance of the Armed Forces of the United States in joint operations and provides the doctrinal basis for interagency coordination and for US military involvement in multinational operations. It provides military guidance for the exercise of authority by combatant commanders and other joint force commanders (JFCs) and prescribes joint doctrine for joint operations, education, and training. It provides military guidance for use by the Armed Forces in preparing their appropriate plans. It is not the intent of this publication to restrict the authority of the JFC from organizing the force and executing the mission in a manner the JFC deems most appropriate to ensure unity of effort in the accomplishment of the overall objective.

3. Application

a. Joint doctrine established in this publication applies to the Joint Staff, commanders of combatant commands, subunified commands, joint task forces, subordinate components of these commands, and the Services.

b. The guidance in this publication is authoritative; as such, this doctrine will be followed except when, in the judgment of the commander, exceptional circumstances dictate otherwise. If conflicts arise between the contents of this publication and the contents of Service publications, this publication will take precedence unless the Chairman of the Joint Chiefs of Staff, normally in coordination with the other members of the Joint Chiefs of Staff, has provided more current and specific guidance. Commanders of forces operating as part of a multinational (alliance or coalition) military command should follow multinational doctrine and procedures ratified by the United States. For doctrine and procedures not ratified by the United States, commanders should evaluate and follow the multinational command's doctrine and procedures, where applicable and consistent with US law, regulations, and doctrine.

For the Chairman of the Joint Chiefs of Staff:

WILLIAM E. GORTNEY
VADM, USN
Director, Joint Staff

Intentionally Blank

SUMMARY OF CHANGES
REVISION OF JOINT PUBLICATION 3-61, DATED 9 MAY 2005

- **Updates the mission of joint public affairs (PA) to better reflect its contribution to joint operations**

- **Amends the responsibilities for the Assistant Secretary of Defense for Public Affairs**

- **Adds an overview of the Deputy Assistant Secretary of Defense for Joint Communication responsibilities**

- **Incorporates an overview of the Defense Media Activity responsibilities**

- **Adopts the term media operations center to represent any type of media support facility instead of joint information bureau or combined press information center**

- **Adds a discussion of the Joint Public Affairs Support Element throughout the document**

- **Discusses capabilities of "visual information" in support of the joint force commander's operational and planning requirements**

- **Adds a discussion of joint PA in domestic operations**

- **Introduces the term "community engagement" replacing the term "community relations"**

- **Addresses "strategic communication," its principles, and how it relates to PA**

- **Adds new appendix describing development and execution of the commander's communications strategy**

- **Establishes the new terms and definitions for inclusion in Joint Publication (JP) 1-02 for community engagement, joint PA support element, and media operations center**

- **Modifies the terms and/or definitions in JP 1-02 for American Forces Radio and Television Service, combat camera, command information, external audience, internal audience, message, PA, public affairs guidance, public diplomacy, public information, security review, and visual information**

- Removes the terms and definitions from JP 1-02 for combat visual information, community relations, community relations program, joint information bureau, and PA ground rules

TABLE OF CONTENTS

EXECUTIVE SUMMARY
COMMANDER'S OVERVIEW

- **Addresses the Military's Obligation to Communicate with the American Public**

- **Discusses Public Affairs (PA) Roles**

- **Delineates the Principles of Information**

- **Lists the Tenets of PA**

- **Discusses PA in Joint Operations**

- **Describes Joint PA in Domestic Situations**

Overview

The First Amendment Guarantees the Freedom of the Press.

The US military has an obligation to communicate with the American public, and it is in the national interest to communicate with the international public. Through the responsive release of accurate information and imagery to domestic and international audiences, public affairs (PA) puts operational actions in context, facilitates the development of informed perceptions about military operations, helps undermine adversarial propaganda efforts, and contributes to the achievement of national, strategic, and operational objectives.

Information Either Contributes or Undermines the Achievement of Operational Objectives.

Information relating to the military and its operations is available to the public from the Department of Defense (DOD) as well as national unofficial sources (e.g., information disseminated by the members, distributed by the public, the media, or by groups hostile to US interests). Regardless of the source, intention or method of distribution, information in the public domain either contributes to or undermines the achievement of operational objectives. Official information can help create, strengthen, or preserve conditions favorable for the advancement of national interests and policies and mitigate any adverse effects from unofficial, misinformed, or hostile sources.

Joint Force Commanders (JFCs) Play a Crucial Role in Successful Public Affairs (PA) Operations.

Official communication with internal and external audiences may have a significant effect on the operational environment. Good planning and message development can have a positive impact on operations. Poor planning and message development can turn operational success into strategic failure. **Credible PA operations support the commander's mission and maintain essential public relationships.**

The Public Affairs Officers (PAOs) are an Integral Part of the Staff.

The public affairs officer (PAO) is the joint force commander's (JFC's) principal spokesperson, senior PA advisor, and member of the personal staff. The PAO must have the resources to provide information and imagery to the JFC, the public, the media, and subordinate and supporting commanders in near real time. PAOs and PA staffs should be involved in planning, decisionmaking, training, equipping, and executing operations as well as integrating PA activities into all levels of the command. This requires them to have the appropriate level clearances to participate in these processes.

PA Roles

PA roles include:

Providing Trusted Counsel to Leaders. This core competency includes anticipating and advising JFCs on the possible impact of military operations and activities within the public information realm.

Enhancing Morale and Readiness. PA activities enable military personnel and their family members to better understand their roles by explaining how policies, programs, and operations affect them.

Fostering Public Trust and Support. Effective PA supports a strong national defense by building public trust and understanding for the military's contribution to national security.

Creating Global Understanding. JFCs should employ PA in concert with other information capabilities to develop and implement communication strategies that inform audiences about the impact of US military during operations.

Supporting the Command Strategy. The synchronization of actions, images, and words leads to the successful execution of command strategy.

Deterring Adversaries. The credible threat of counteraction is a deterrent to adversary action. PA assists combatant commanders in planning deterrence efforts and disseminates information and imagery to convey to the adversary possible countermeasures, potentially avoiding the need to use force.

Principles of Information

It is the responsibility of DOD to **make available timely and accurate information so that the public, Congress, and the news media may assess and understand facts about national security and defense strategy.** Requests for information from organizations and private citizens shall be answered quickly. In carrying out DOD policy, the following DOD principles of information shall apply:

Information shall be made fully and readily available, consistent with statutory requirements, unless its release is precluded by national security constraints or valid statutory mandates or exceptions. The provisions of the Freedom of Information Act will be supported in both letter and spirit.

A free flow of general and military information shall be made available, without censorship or propaganda, to the men and women of the Armed Forces of the United States, including civilian employees, contractors, and their dependents.

Information **will not be classified or otherwise withheld to protect the government from criticism or embarrassment.**

Information shall be withheld **only when disclosure would adversely affect national security or threaten the safety or privacy of the men and women of the Armed Forces.**

DOD's obligation to provide the public with information **may require coordination with other government agencies (OGAs).** Such activity is to expedite the flow of information to the public.

Propaganda has no place in DOD PA programs.

Tenets of PA

Effective application of the PA tenets normally results in more effective and efficient execution of PA operations and relationships with the media. They complement the DOD principles of information and describe best practices. The tenets should be reviewed and appropriately applied during all stages of joint operation planning and execution. The tenets are:

Tell the Truth. JFC's PA personnel will release only accurate information of officially released information.

Provide Timely Information and Imagery. Commanders should be prepared to release timely, factual, coordinated, and approved information and imagery about military operations.

Practice Security at the Source. All DOD personnel and DOD contractors are responsible for safeguarding sensitive information.

Provide Consistent Information at All Levels. The public often receives simultaneous information from a variety of official DOD sources at various levels.

Tell the DOD Story. Although commanders designate only military personnel or DOD civilian employees as official spokespersons, they should educate and encourage all their military, civilian employees, and contractors to tell the DOD story by providing them with timely information that is appropriate for public release.

Mission, Responsibilities, and Relationships

PA Mission

The mission of joint PA is to plan, coordinate, and synchronize US military public information activities and resources in order to support the commander's intent and concept of operations.

PAO Responsibilities

The PAO advises the JFC on the implications of command decisions, actions, and operations on foreign and domestic public perceptions and plans, executes, and evaluates PA activities and events to support overall operational success. PA is also responsible, in conjunction with information operations, for generating the information requirements to assess the public perceptions of foreign audiences, and integrating that information into mission planning.

Responsibility and Benefits of Communicating

US civilian and military leadership is accountable and responsible to the American people for supporting and defending national interests worldwide. By providing accurate and timely information, imagery, and clear explanations of its activities, DOD contributes to the public's understanding of military operations. JFCs must recognize their responsibility to communicate with the American people and the benefits of communicating with international audiences.

Public Affairs in Joint Operations

PA Functions

PA activities are divided into public information, command information, and community engagement supported by planning and analysis and assessment throughout the course of operations.

PA Requirements

PA activities require facilities, personnel, equipment, transportation assets, and communication capabilities. Anticipated PA resource requirements should be identified and addressed as early in the planning process as possible, since PA requirements often exceed available resources. Planning considers specific measures to augment PA personnel and procure, lease, or assign other necessary resources. This generally requires assistance from the supporting combatant commands, Services, and the military departments.

PA Planning

PA planners establish and maintain a routine, ongoing relationship with other planners within the combatant command and joint task force. Synchronization across the staff facilitates the availability of services and support required to execute PA activities. **PA planning should include coordination with the host nation, the country team, OGAs, intergovernmental organizations, and nongovernmental organizations, as appropriate.**

PA Planning Considerations

During initial planning it is critical to synchronize PA planning and activities across the joint force and with other agencies as necessary. Authorities to plan, integrate, approve, and disseminate appropriate information and imagery should be clearly established. Legal considerations regarding release of information on investigations in the joint operations area, including those regarding alleged law of war violations, should be addressed as early as possible in the public affairs guidance (PAG). Coordination of overall themes, as well as a plan to support media coverage and all applicable PAG, should be approved prior to hostilities in order to effectively shape the information environment.

PA Support for Specific Operations

Commanders should ensure PA activities are tailored to support the joint forces across the range of military operations. While the public and the media are interested in the essential facts of any situation, that information is incomplete without an understanding of the background, underlying rationale, and other fundamental elements particular to a certain type of operation. Experience shows that media interest in civil support, foreign humanitarian assistance, managing the consequences of incidents, peace operations, and similar operations often peaks early, then diminishes gradually. PA planning should take this into account.

There is a Need for Continuous Dialogue between the Joint Force and the Media.

Open and independent reporting are the principal means of coverage of military operations. Commanders should seek regular opportunities to work with the media. Media coverage of potential future military operations can, to a large extent, shape public perception of the joint force and national security environment. Thus, JFCs and their PAOs continually assess their understanding of the direct and indirect effects of potential actions and signals on perceptions, attitudes, and beliefs, and should formulate and deliver timely and culturally attuned messages.

PA personnel should act as liaisons but should not interfere with the reporting process. The PA mission includes helping media representatives understand joint force events and occurrences so that media coverage is accurate. The JFC, or a designated representative, should conduct frequent operational briefings to inform internal and external audiences of current military operations and respond to media questions.

The Criteria for Credentialing Journalists are Established by the Joint Force PAO or the media operations

Credentialing is not intended to be a control measure or means to restrict certain media outlets from access. It is primarily a method of validating individuals as journalists and providing them with information that enhances their ability to report on activities within the operational area.

centers (MOCs) Director.	Credentialing media representatives also ensures that, if captured, they are recognized as journalists and treated accordingly under the law of war.
Ground Rules	**Ground rules** are developed to protect members of DOD from the release of information that could threaten their security or safety during ongoing operations yet facilitates the media's access to timely, relevant information. Ground rules reconcile the desire of the media to cover military operations with DOD security and safety concerns and are in no way intended to prevent release of derogatory, embarrassing, negative, or noncomplimentary information. Media ground rules include requirements designed to protect the security, health, and welfare of the media.
The Joint Force PAO is Responsible to the JFC for Directing PA Activities.	The joint force PAO, with appropriate staff support, is on the commander's personal staff and is directly responsible for all the JFC's PA requirements. The joint force PAO provides PA counsel and support to the commander and provides oversight of all the PA functions and subordinate media operations centers (MOCs). The MOC director, with supporting MOC staff, is responsible for coordinating all media operations within the operational area, and provides and coordinates support to the JFC through the joint force PAO.
The Early Establishment of MOCs is an Important Step in the Responsive and Efficient Facilitation of Media Operations.	Media operations may be the sole purview of a MOC or conducted by a media operations section; the requirements remain basically the same. A MOC is the central point of contact between the military and media representatives covering operations. It offers a venue for commanders and PA staffs to discuss their units and their roles in the joint operation and helps journalists obtain information quickly and efficiently on a wide variety of complex activities. It should be staffed to support local and regional non-English speaking media. It may also support command information activities.

Joint Public Affairs in Domestic Operations

The Conduct of PA in Domestic Operations is Somewhat Different for Department of Defense.	By Homeland Security Presidential Directive-5, DOD PA operates in accordance with guidance in the National Response Framework incident communications emergency policy and procedures, which provides detailed guidance to all federal incident communicators during a federal response to an event. It establishes mechanisms to

prepare and deliver coordinated and sustained messages, and provides for prompt federal acknowledgement of an incident and communication of emergency information to the public.

Domestic Operations are Planned and Executed in Three Phases

DOD PA support evolves as follows:

Shaping. The DOD is rarely a "first responder" for domestic situations. In this phase PA manages expectations regarding DOD's response among both the public and the other responding agencies. PA activities include developing themes and messages that clearly explain the scope and timing of the DOD response.

Engagement. This is the phase where military forces are actually on-scene supporting an incident and PA is actively informing the public about DOD activities via releases of information and imagery, press conferences, and site visits.

Transition. This is the phase where military forces begin to disengage from incident response support. It is critical that PA activities in this phase articulate why DOD support is no longer required.

Joint Information Center (JIC)

A substantial portion of the overall PA effort will be supporting the media to ensure affected populations are receiving necessary information. In order to coordinate the timely release of emergency/incident-related information, imagery, and other PA functions, a joint information center (JIC) may be established.

JIC Location

The JIC is normally **located close to the best sources of information** about the situation, such as an incident command post or emergency operations center. Note that DOD and other agencies will often have a separate staff performing PA duties/functions on behalf of their own agency. In the absence of a JIC, coordination still needs to occur between DOD, other agencies, and the primary agency.

CONCLUSION

This publication provides fundamental principles and guidance for PA support to joint operations. It also addresses PA operations and the role of PA in strategic communication. It adds a discussion of joint PA in domestic operations.

Intentionally Blank

CHAPTER I
OVERVIEW

THE CHALLENGE

"...I say to you: That we are in battle, and more than half of this battle is taking place in the battlefield of the media. And that we are in a media battle in a race for the hearts and minds of our Umma..."

Ayman al-Zawahiri to Abu Musa al-Zarqawi, 2005

1. Introduction

   a. The US military has an obligation to communicate with the American public, and it is in the national interest to communicate with the international public. Through the responsive release of accurate information and imagery to domestic and international audiences, public affairs (PA) puts operational actions in context, facilitates the development of informed perceptions about military operations, helps undermine adversarial propaganda efforts, and contributes to the achievement of national, strategic, and operational objectives.

   b. The First Amendment guarantees freedom of the press, but this right must be balanced against the military mission that requires operations security (OPSEC). The military's operational mission requires that OPSEC be practiced at all levels of command to protect the lives of American or multinational forces and the security of ongoing or future operations. These competing goals sometimes lead to friction between the media and the military.

THE MEDIA AND THE MILITARY

"Today, I want to encourage you always to remember the importance of the two pillars of our freedom under the Constitution: the Congress and the press. Both surely try our patience from time to time, but they are the surest guarantees of the liberty of the American people."

Secretary of Defense Robert Gates
Speech at the 2007 US Naval Academy Graduation

   c. The tempo of military operations, OPSEC concerns, and the number and variety of other information sources competing for the attention of the populace complicate the joint force commanders' (JFCs') ability to provide accurate information to internal and external audiences at the same pace as the media and other sources release their perspective on a usually sensational and emotional event. The ability of anyone with Internet access to communicate and provide graphic visuals as an event unfolds, often without validating facts, further complicates the military's effort to accurately inform the media and populace. JFCs and public affairs officers (PAOs) should evaluate missions to identify information and imagery requirements, as well as the means to acquire and move those products in a timely manner. PA planning should include considerations to reduce the time lag between an event and what can be communicated.

d. Information relating to the military and its operations is available to the public from the Department of Defense (DOD) as well as unofficial sources (e.g., information disseminated by Service members, distributed by the public, the media, or by groups hostile to US interests). Regardless of the source, intention or method of distribution, information in the public domain either contributes to or undermines the achievement of operational objectives. Official information can help create, strengthen, or preserve conditions favorable for the advancement of national interests and policies and mitigate any adverse effects from unofficial, misinformed, or hostile sources.

e. JFCs play a crucial role in successful PA operations. Official communication with internal and external audiences may have a significant effect on the operational environment. Good planning and message development can have a positive impact on operations. Poor planning and message development can turn operational success into strategic failure. Credible PA operations support the commander's mission and maintain essential public relationships.

f. The PAO is the JFC's principal spokesperson, senior PA advisor, and member of the personal staff. The PAO must have the resources to provide information and imagery to the JFC, the public, the media, and subordinate and supporting commanders in near real time. PAOs and PA staffs should be involved in planning, decisionmaking, training, equipping, and executing operations as well as integrating PA activities into all levels of the command. This requires them to have the appropriate level clearances to participate in these processes.

g. Public support for the US military's presence or operations is not uniform throughout the operational area. The PAO must provide the JFC with an assessment of public support within the operational area and provide feedback on trends in public opinion based on media analysis, published polling data, and professional assessments.

2. Public Affairs and the Operational Environment

a. **General.** Information in the public domain impacts the operational environment. Commanders need to understand the relationship between the physical and information components and the impact various friendly, adversary, and neutral actions, images, and words have on the operational environment.

b. **The Pervasive Backdrop.** Information is the pervasive backdrop to the operational environment and is continuously changing. Plans and operational decisions are driven by the constant monitoring, assessment, and analysis of the information environment. The operational environment is saturated; signals compete for the attention of their audiences, so it is important for the joint force to coordinate its messages—and to integrate those messages with its partners' as part of the ongoing synchronization to maintain unity of effort.

For additional guidance on the operational environment, see Joint Publication (JP) 3-0, Joint Operations.

(1) **Preeminence of Information.** The power of first impressions on the perceptions and attitudes of decisionmakers, leaders, and other individuals should not be underestimated. The timeliness of information is a recognized element of news (see Figure I-1.) Adversaries take advantage of the speed with which information travels and can often communicate lies or misleading information faster than we can communicate the truth. First impressions influence later perceptions and judgments and also bias how information received later is processed. Additionally, information that contradicts first impressions may be dismissed all together. Traditionally, the US military has been hesitant to release information that is incomplete or to acknowledge events until a fairly good level of granularity is available. The information environment is in a constant state of flux, and the JFCs should be prepared to assume some risk in order to ensure that public communication activities can be executed in time to ensure the most accurate and contextual information is publicly available.

(2) **Recency and Repetition.** Recency is a key component of what makes information newsworthy. It is also a factor in information retention as is repetition of the information being provided. It is not always enough to simply make a public statement. For information to be effectively processed, individuals must receive the information in a timely fashion, multiple times, and from multiple sources. Continuous public engagement throughout an operation provides the best chance of success in supporting strategic communication (SC) themes and in achieving operational objectives.

(3) **The Influence of Culture.** News is considered a cultural narrative produced by people who generally espouse and adhere to the values and cultural system of the society they serve. Ideology often provides the framework through which events are represented. Media coverage does not always reflect reality, but frames reality by choosing what events to cover and how to present them. The world looks different to people because the information they receive is influenced by their ideology, ethnocentricity, and culture. Consideration of the impact of culture on how news and information is presented and on how that then affects

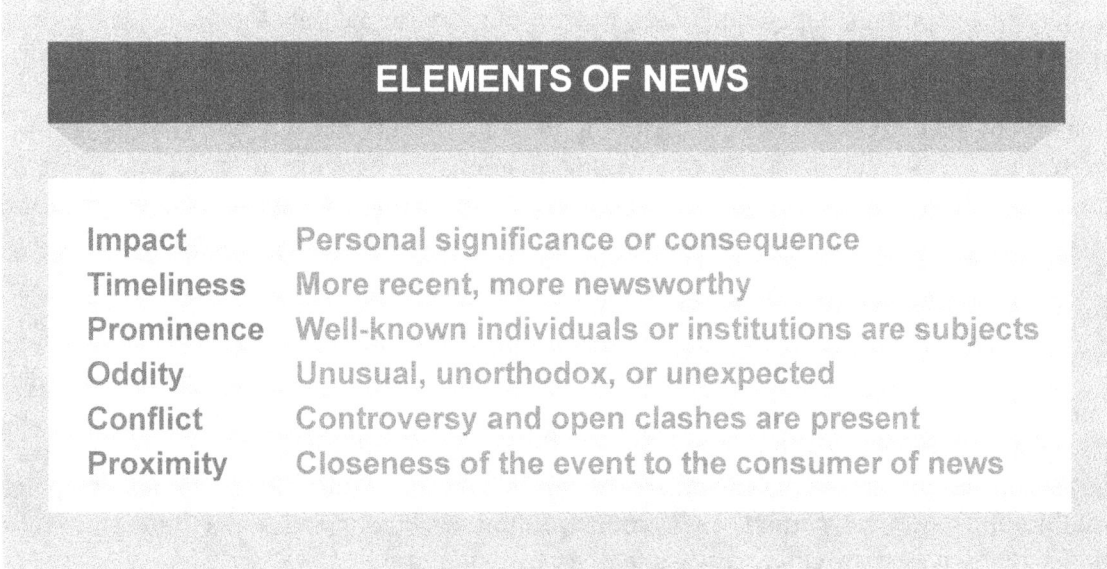

ELEMENTS OF NEWS

Impact   Personal significance or consequence
Timeliness   More recent, more newsworthy
Prominence   Well-known individuals or institutions are subjects
Oddity   Unusual, unorthodox, or unexpected
Conflict   Controversy and open clashes are present
Proximity   Closeness of the event to the consumer of news

Figure I-1. Elements of News

> *"The emotionally gripping pictures of the war had a huge impact on Egyptian viewers. Egyptian families became emotionally involved, expressing waves of rage, disgust, and anger at seeing pictures of Iraqi bodies torn to pieces littered everywhere, bloodshed, and the destruction of Arab cities and population centers. The image of an American flag draped over Saddam Hussein's statue was transmitted to tens of millions of Arab viewers and contributed to a sense of the humiliation of their Arab brothers and their fears of American imperialism. This is an excellent example of the power of transnational satellite broadcasts—one soldier makes an individual gesture and an entire region watches in astonishment."*
>
> **Hussein Amin**
> **Senior Editor**
> **Transnational Broadcasting Studies**
> **"Watching the War" in the Arab World**
> **No. 10, Spring/Summer 2003**

information consumers must become second nature. Attempts to mitigate the impact of actions on public opinion after the fact are often ineffective.

(4) **Impact of Propaganda.** Propaganda is any form of adversary communication, especially of a biased or misleading nature, designed to influence the opinions, emotions, attitudes, or behavior of any group in order to benefit the sponsor, either directly or indirectly. The traditional factors that make information about an event newsworthy are the same factors that make propaganda compelling. People are drawn to conflict or violence, and our adversaries have mastered the art of using it, real and contrived, to influence information consumers to further their objectives and minimize our effectiveness. Anticipating those actions that the adversary may exploit with propaganda and limiting that potential with preemptive release of information is paramount. When operations do not allow for such actions, being prepared to respond quickly to counter propaganda is critical.

c. **PA is Critical across the Range of Military Operations.** The United States employs military capabilities to support national security goals at home and abroad in a variety of operations. Operations vary in size, purpose, and combat intensity that extend from military engagement, security cooperation, and deterrence activities to crisis response and limited contingency operations and, if necessary, major operations and campaigns. PA is inherent in all military activities spanning the range of military operations as depicted in Figure I-2. It is a key enabler for managing and delivering public information on a daily basis as well as supporting military operations. A synchronized and coordinated PA effort with interagency partners can facilitate success in other military operations.

3. **Public Affairs Roles**

a. **Providing Trusted Counsel to Leaders.** This core competency includes anticipating and advising JFCs on the possible impact of military operations and activities within the public information realm. This also includes preparing JFCs to communicate with audiences through the media and other methods of communication, as well as analyzing and interpreting the information environment, monitoring domestic and foreign public understanding, and providing lessons learned from the past.

Figure I-2. Public Affairs across the Range of Military Operations

b. **Enhancing Morale and Readiness.** PA activities enable military personnel and their family members to better understand their roles by explaining how policies, programs, and operations affect them. Uncertainty and concern regarding living conditions in the operational area and at home, the duration of separation, the lack of daily communications between family members, and many other factors impact morale and readiness at home and within the unit. PA activities can help alleviate some of these issues. PA activities can also counter adversary propaganda efforts and address incomplete or misinformed media reports, thus reducing the stress and uncertainty felt by Service members and their families. Additionally, as media interest expands to include "human interest stories," military personnel and family members can expect the media to cover the impact of military operations on their lives and livelihood, to include their daily activities. Family members, including spouses and children, may be approached for interviews. This will have a direct and indirect impact on morale. PA's ability to assist Service members and their families in understanding how to deal with the media and to assist in providing relevant and responsive information on topical issues requires planning and resources and should be incorporated into the command's planning efforts.

c. **Fostering Public Trust and Support.** Effective PA supports a strong national defense by building public trust and understanding for the military's contribution to national security. PA gives the American public the information needed to understand military roles and missions. This understanding is critical to sustaining American public support for military operations.

d. **Creating Global Understanding.** JFCs should employ PA in concert with other information capabilities to develop and implement communication strategies that inform audiences about the impact of US military during operations. Making these audiences aware of US military capabilities and US resolve to employ them can enhance support from allies and friendly countries.

e. **Supporting the Command Strategy.** The synchronization of actions, images, and words leads to the successful execution of command strategy. PA can provide a continuous flow of credible, reliable, timely, and accurate information and imagery to internal and external audiences. This capability allows PA to help deter efforts to diminish national will, degrade morale, and turn world opinion against friendly operations. PA must be engaged in operational planning, have access to open source reports and relevant intelligence, understand common adversary propaganda techniques, and be very aggressive in anticipating adversary propaganda—putting accurate information out first so that friendly forces gain the initiative and remain the preferred source of information. Gaining and maintaining the information initiative in a conflict can help discredit and undermine adversary propaganda. The first side that presents the information sets the context and frames the public debate. It is extremely important to get accurate information and imagery out first—even information that portrays DOD in a negative manner. This helps disarm the adversary's propaganda and defeats attempts by the adversary to use these mistakes against friendly forces. Credibility must be maintained. PA professionals require the knowledge, skills, resources, capabilities, and authority to rapidly release information, in accordance with DOD policy and guidance, to various publics to effectively support the command strategy.

f. **Deterring Adversaries.** The credible threat of counteraction is a deterrent to adversary action. PA assists combatant commanders (CCDRs) in planning deterrence efforts and disseminates information and imagery to convey to the adversary possible countermeasures, potentially avoiding the need to use force. PA clearly communicates US military goals and objectives, what we expect the adversary to do to satisfy international concerns, why the US concern is important, and what the US intends to do if the adversary refuses to comply. Additionally, adversary propaganda frequently targets the resolve of the American public. PA's counterpropaganda efforts are aimed at informing the American public of this threat and affirming its trust in and resolve with the Armed Forces. PA activities may involve highlighting the military's deployment preparations, activities, and force projection to show the domestic, multinational, and adversary public what the commander is actually doing to prepare for conflict. When adversaries are not deterred from conflict, information about US capabilities and resolve may still shape the adversary's planning and actions in a manner beneficial to the US.

4. Public Affairs Fundamentals

a. **Principles of Information.** It is the responsibility of DOD to make available timely and accurate information so that the public, Congress, and the news media may assess and understand facts about national security and defense strategy. Requests for information from organizations and private citizens shall be answered quickly. In carrying out DOD policy, the following DOD principles of information shall apply:

(1) Information shall be made fully and readily available, consistent with statutory requirements, unless its release is precluded by national security constraints or valid statutory mandates or exceptions. The provisions of the Freedom of Information Act will be supported in both letter and spirit.

(2) A free flow of general and military information shall be made available, without censorship or propaganda, to the men and women of the Armed Forces of the United States, including civilian employees, contractors, and their dependents.

(3) Information will not be classified or otherwise withheld to protect the government from criticism or embarrassment.

(4) Information shall be withheld only when disclosure would adversely affect national security or threaten the safety or privacy of the men and women of the Armed Forces.

(5) DOD's obligation to provide the public with information may require coordination with other government agencies (OGAs). Such activity is to expedite the flow of information to the public.

(6) Propaganda has no place in DOD PA programs.

b. **Tenets of Public Affairs.** Effective application of the PA tenets described below normally result in more effective and efficient execution of PA operations and relationships with the media. They complement the DOD principles of information discussed above and describe best practices. The tenets should be reviewed and appropriately applied during all stages of joint operation planning and execution.

(1) **Tell the Truth.** JFC's PA personnel will release only accurate information. The long-term success of PA operations depends on maintaining the integrity and credibility of officially released information. Deceiving the public undermines trust in the Armed Forces. Accurate, balanced, credible presentation of information leads to confidence in the Armed Forces and the legitimacy of operations. Attempting to deny unfavorable information or failing to acknowledge its existence leads to media speculation, the perception of cover-up, and lost public trust. These issues should be openly and honestly addressed as soon as possible.

(2) **Provide Timely Information and Imagery.** Commanders should be prepared to release timely, factual, coordinated, and approved information and imagery about military operations. Information and imagery introduced into the public realm has a powerful effect

on friendly, neutral, and adversary decision-making cycles and perceptions. The source that releases more timely and accurate information and imagery often enjoys the benefit of becoming the media's preferred source of information. PAOs need to establish expeditious processes for release of information.

(3) **Practice Security at the Source.** All DOD personnel and DOD contractors are responsible for safeguarding sensitive information. As sources of information, each DOD member should be aware of OPSEC issues, whether being interviewed by the media or sharing information and imagery with family or friends including through social media. Therefore, it is important that official information and imagery be approved for release prior to dissemination to the public.

(4) **Provide Consistent Information at All Levels.** The public often receives simultaneous information from a variety of official DOD sources at various levels. When this information is conflicting, DOD's credibility is put in jeopardy. Information and imagery must be appropriately coordinated and in compliance with official DOD and the supported commander's guidance before it is released to the public.

(5) **Tell the DOD Story.** Although commanders designate only military personnel or DOD civilian employees as official spokespersons, they should educate and encourage all their military, civilian employees, and contractors to tell the DOD story by providing them with timely information that is appropriate for public release. By projecting confidence and commitment during interviews or in talking to family and friends, DOD personnel can help promote public understanding of military operations and activities.

c. **Audiences**

(1) **American Public.** Commanders have an obligation to inform the American public about their nation's military. This communication enhances morale and readiness and increases public trust and support. Through active engagement, the military demonstrates it is a community partner and a responsible steward of national resources.

(2) **International.** Current information technology allows information and imagery to be available worldwide. International interest in military operations may be just as high, and sometimes higher, than US media interest, especially in military operations conducted overseas. DOD, in coordination with Department of State (DOS), host, and partner nations, should keep the international community informed about US military operations and activities within the constraints of OPSEC.

(3) **Internal.** Command information programs are the primary means commanders use to communicate with military members, DOD civilian employees, contractors, and family members. As used in this document, military members include Active Component (AC), Reserve Component (RC) (which includes the National Guard), as well as retired officers and enlisted personnel.

(4) **Adversaries.** PA distributes timely, truthful, and accurate information regarding US intentions and actions to adversary audiences to counter misinformation, disinformation, and propaganda and to deter adversary actions. It is critical that PA and

information operations (IO), especially military information support operations (MISO), synchronize their communications efforts with respect to the adversary due to the fluidity of the information environment.

5. **Public Affairs and Strategic Communication**

a. SC requires the integration and synchronization of actions, images, and words in order to communicate desired themes and messages in support of greater US and DOD objectives. SC is focused United States Government (USG) efforts to understand and engage key audiences to create, strengthen, or preserve conditions favorable for the advancement of USG interests, policies, and objectives through the use of coordinated programs, plans, themes, messages, and products synchronized with the actions of all instruments of national power. DOD supports the principles of SC in Figure I-3.

b. As an SC primary capability, PA activities are coordinated and synchronized with all other activities (visual information [VI], defense support to public diplomacy [DSPD], IO, and operational actions).

c. SC planning must be integrated into military planning and operations, documented in operation plans (OPLANs) or operation orders (OPORDs), and coordinated and synchronized with OGAs and multinational partners. Use of synchronized themes, messages, images, and actions by the joint force can be critical to mission accomplishment. SC includes national activities not under the direct control of the JFC, adding complexity for

PRINCIPLES OF STRATEGIC COMMUNICATION

Leaders Must Lead Communication Process

Credible
Perception of truthfulness and respect

Dialogue
Multifaceted exchange of ideas

Unity of Effort
Integrated and coordinated

Responsive
Right audience, message, time, and place

Understanding
Deep comprehension of others

Pervasive
Every action sends a message

Results-based
Tied to desired end state

Continuous
Analysis, planning, execution, and assessment

Figure I-3. Principles of Strategic Communication

> *"General Petraeus understood the power of messaging. He knew that at times a message sent by our actions had much more impact than a carefully crafted sound bite delivered at a press conference. He also understood that our words sometimes led our actions. Regardless, our communication efforts helped put into proper context, characterization, and accuracy the actions we took."*
>
> **Rear Admiral Greg Smith, US Navy**
> **Director of Communications**
> **US Central Command**
> **September 2008**

planning and execution. Using approved SC themes requires conscious and collaborative coordination. Assessment measures, methods, and resources must be developed and incorporated in planning and execution. Measuring progress toward mission accomplishment assists commanders in decisionmaking and adjusting operations to achieve military objectives and reach the desired end state.

d. Communication objectives and efforts should be fully integrated in command operational planning and execution processes, so there is consistency in intent between command actions and information disseminated about those actions. The JFC, as part of the SC effort, should ensure planning for PA, IO, and DSPD is coordinated to make certain consistent themes and messages are communicated that support the overall USG SC objectives. Some commanders use the commander's communications strategy model to ensure their communication activities are nested with actions and strategies at all levels. Messages should support themes at each level and should support (or be nested under) the next higher-level themes. Themes at all levels should support strategic and national level objectives. This ensures consistent communications to global audiences. Appendix A, "Commander's Communications Strategy," provides additional detail.

e. The operational environment is influenced by a combination of actions, images, and words. The increasing transparency of military operations resulting from the nearly continuous media coverage and the growing use of personal communication devices to document events puts US forces and their actions under constant scrutiny. It can turn a seemingly innocuous tactical incident into one of strategic significance. If the escalation of an action does not occur on its own, adversaries have proven adept perception of a crisis to force us into a reactive posture. Commanders must be as involved in shaping the information narrative as they are in planning and conducting operations. Carefully planned communication objectives and efforts are key to this effort. Official information released in a timely manner—in some cases ahead of military action—can put operational actions into context and help counter enemy propaganda. What US forces do is often more important in terms of influencing the operational environment than what DOD conveys with official information.

CHAPTER II
MISSION, RESPONSIBILITIES, AND RELATIONSHIPS

"Public sentiment is everything. With public sentiment, nothing can fail; without it, nothing can succeed."

Abraham Lincoln
Lincoln-Douglas Debate at Ottawa
21 August 1858

1. Mission

a. The mission of joint PA is to plan, coordinate, and synchronize US military public information activities and resources in order to support the commander's intent and concept of operations (CONOPS). The PAO advises the JFC on the implications of command decisions, actions, and operations on foreign and domestic public perceptions and plans, executes, and evaluates PA activities and events to support overall operational success. PA is also responsible, in conjunction with IO, for generating the information requirements to assess the public perceptions of foreign audiences, and integrating that information into mission planning.

b. US civilian and military leadership is accountable and responsible to the American people for supporting and defending national interests worldwide. By providing accurate and timely information, imagery, and clear explanations of its activities, DOD contributes to the public's understanding of military operations. JFCs must recognize their responsibility to communicate with the American people and the benefits of communicating with international audiences. Even with the proliferation of information sources, traditional media are still the principal means of communicating with the public. The Internet also provides numerous options and challenges for unfiltered communications with various audiences.

(1) JFCs must recognize the changing nature of how people get information. The speed and methods with which people and organizations can collect and convey information to the public makes it possible for the world populace to quickly become aware of military activity. Internet sites have become our adversaries' preferred means to engage global audiences. This instantaneous, unfiltered, biased, and often incomplete or factually incorrect information requires PA to be operationally nimble to help disarm the adversaries' efforts with fast, complete, factual, and credible information.

(2) The joint force PA staff should develop well-defined and concise plans to help accomplish operational objectives and minimize the adverse effects of inaccurate information and analysis, and counter propaganda and the spread of disinformation and misinformation while taking OPSEC considerations into account. Well-planned PA activities should be incorporated in every phase of joint operations. Any PA CONOPS should provide open, independent reporting and dissemination of information with maximum disclosure and minimum delay, as well as create an environment that encourages balanced coverage of operations. Commanders need to determine the lowest level authority in which

US FIGHTS AN INFORMATION WAR IN AFGHANISTAN

BAGRAM AIR BASE, AFGHANISTAN—The accusation was damning: US soldiers were said to have tossed a grenade into a crowd of Afghans in the eastern province of Kunar on Tuesday, killing two civilians and wounding five to 50 others.

American public affairs officers previously have been slow in responding. US military officials here complain that Taliban leaders are often better and faster at spreading their versions of deadly events.

This time, however, public affairs officers mounted a swift and detailed information operation. Within 24 hours, a public affairs team at Bagram air base released a video showing an explosion as US soldiers worked to free an American military vehicle stuck on a median in the town of Asadabad. It also provided technical details it said proved the grenade was a Russian-made version commonly used by insurgents.

It is not clear from the murky video, taken at a distance, who threw the grenade. But no American soldier is seen throwing anything.

The unusually rapid release of the video was clearly intended to show that American soldiers working on a marooned vehicle were hardly likely to detonate a grenade next to their own vehicles and comrades, three of whom were slightly wounded.

The video was posted on Facebook and YouTube, part of a burgeoning US effort to use social networking sites to build support for coalition forces locked in a struggle to win over the Afghan population in the face of an entrenched Islamic insurgency. The US military regularly issues statements denying accusations of misconduct, but release of combat videos has been rare.

The overnight posting of the video underscores the long-held belief within the US military that it needs to be faster and more sophisticated in responding to false allegations...

David Zucchino
Los Angeles Times, 11 June 2009

information can be released to ensure timeliness. Release should be in accordance with DOD policy and guidance.

2. **Responsibilities**

   a. **Assistant Secretary of Defense for Public Affairs (ASD[PA]):**

      (1) Determines who should serve as the initial source of release of information about joint, multinational, and certain single-service operations and delegates PA release authority to the appropriate commander as soon as practical.

(2) Approves and disseminates PA guidance (PAG), PA plans, and PA annexes.

(3) Facilitates deployment of the DOD Media Pool as required.

(4) Oversees the employment of joint combat camera (COMCAM) teams and the distribution of their products, including follow-on use/release of still and motion pictures supporting operations including PA, as established in Department of Defense Instruction (DODI) 5040.4, *Joint Combat Camera (COMCAM) Program.*

(5) Establishes, as necessary, a crisis and/or wartime PA cell at the Pentagon.

(6) Facilitates the deployment of American Forces Radio and Television Service (AFRTS) resources and equipment, for command information programs as established in Department of Defense Directive (DODD) 5120.20, *American Forces Radio and Television Service (AFRTS),* and DOD, 5120.20R, *Management and Operation of American Forces Radio and Television Service.*

(7) Coordinates PA policy with the Chairman of the Joint Chiefs of Staff (CJCS), the Military Departments, combatant commands, and political or military authorities within host nations (HNs), alliances, and coalitions.

(8) Ensures PAG contained in CJCS warning, planning, alert, deployment, and execute orders (EXORDs) is in accordance with established guidance and intent. May provide periodic US military training, familiarization training, and education to accredited national and international media to support media embed programs with operational units.

(9) Supports deployed PA staffs with media analysis.

Additional responsibilities and guidance are contained in DODD 5122.05, Assistant Secretary of Defense for Public Affairs (ASD[PA]), *and DODI 5400.13,* Public Affairs (PA) Operations.

b. **The Deputy Assistant Secretary of Defense for Joint Communication:**

(1) Focuses on two major mission areas—SC, which includes future communication planning and coordination within DOD, and joint PA oversight, which includes helping ensure DOD's PA capabilities are properly organized, trained, and equipped.

(2) Prepare SC proposals and products for review by the Deputy Secretary of Defense and Secretary of Defense (SecDef), as required.

c. **The Director, Defense Media Activity (DMA).** The DMA is a DOD field activity created by the consolidation of the Army Broadcasting Service, Soldiers Radio/Television (TV), Soldiers Media Center, Naval Media Center, Air Force Public Affairs Agency, American Forces Information Service (AFIS), and the Joint Hometown News Service.

DEFENSE INFORMATION SCHOOL
THE CENTER OF EXCELLENCE FOR VISUAL INFORMATION
AND PUBLIC AFFAIRS

The Defense Information School (DINFOS), located at Fort George G. Meade, Maryland, is the Department of Defense (DOD)-directed school that conducts career-long training and development of public affairs (PA) and visual information (VI) professionals. Its mission is to grow and sustain a corps of professional organizational communicators capable of fulfilling the needs of military leaders and audiences under the most demanding operational conditions. Instruction is given to DOD officers, enlisted personnel, and civilian employees. Limited class space is available for civilian employees of other US Government departments and international officers. Resident courses offer entry level and advanced training in courses covering PA, journalism, broadcasting, broadcast systems maintenance, graphics, electronic imaging, photojournalism, video production, and VI management. Also, organizational communicators receive professional support through the school's web site (www.dinfos.osd.mil). There, they can access distance learning courses, search PA-focused databases, or request professional guidance from DINFOS faculty and staff.

Various Sources

(1) Provides information products to DOD and external audiences through all available media, including motion and still imagery, print, radio, TV, Internet, and related communication technologies.

(2) Provides US radio and TV news, information, and entertainment programming to military Service members, DOD civilians, and contract employees and their families overseas and on board Navy and Coast Guard ships and other authorized users.

(3) Provides joint education and training for military and civilian PA/visual information (VI) personnel at the Defense Information School (DINFOS).

For more information on how to access DMA services, see Appendix D, "Sources for Defense Media Activity," *and DODD 5105.74*, Defense Media Activity.

d. **The Secretaries of the Military Departments:**

(1) Develop PA policies and Service doctrine and provide resources (personnel and standardized and/or compatible equipment) necessary. Ensure the immediate readiness and prompt availability of necessary AC and RC PA resources to support any assigned mission and validated requests for PA augmentation by CCDRs.

(2) Organize, train, equip, and provide AC/RC PA and VI personnel and units to conduct PA activities in support of CCDRs. Personnel should be trained to function in domestic, joint, and multinational environments and should receive predeployment training tailored to the specific needs of the operation.

(3) Conduct Service-specific PA programs, as required, in support of joint and multinational operations.

(4) Should consider the appropriate security clearance levels necessary for PA and VI personnel, including RC augmentees, to participate in the appropriate operational planning, execution, and assessment processes.

e. **The Chairman of the Joint Chiefs of Staff:**

(1) Promulgates joint PA doctrine.

(2) Ensures that existing and new PA annexes to joint operation and exercise plans and orders prepared by the CCDRs comply with published joint PA doctrine, policy, and regulations.

(3) Provides a PA representative to augment the National Military Command Center response cells during times of crisis and conflict to serve as Joint Staff liaison on PA activities to ASD(PA).

(4) Supports DOD in explaining various aspects of joint operations by providing senior officers with the necessary expertise and experience to communicate with the media and internal and external audiences.

(5) Provides PA coordination and planning assistance for the DOD Media Pool deployment.

(6) Ensures CJCS warning, planning, alert, deployment, and EXORDs contain appropriate PA guidance paragraphs.

f. **The Combatant Commanders:**

(1) Coordinate and, when appropriate, synchronize the SC primary communication supporting capabilities.

(2) Develop detailed PA annexes, coordinated and synchronized with SC guidance and associated capabilities, to OPLANS to ensure that foundational SC guidance, including and in support of greater DOD/USG objectives, is available for communication efforts. Develop detailed PA annexes to OPLANs to ensure that required PA support is available.

(a) Conduct appropriate planning for priority in-theater air and ground transportation for movement of media representatives, military personnel supporting the PA mission (may include PA, VI, and COMCAM personnel), the media, and their equipment.

(b) Develop plans to provide for appropriate PA resources and establish priorities for the movement of PA assets.

(c) Develop plans to provide for appropriate communications assets, including Internet access and/or satellite or mobile telephones for the deploying PA staff and AFRTS, if applicable, as well as for use by the media if no other means of communications exist.

(3) Consider bandwidth and other communications/information technology requirements. Commanders should prioritize requirements and allocate resources based on their intent, CONOPS, available resources, and the operational environment.

(4) Plan for the support of media representatives and military personnel supporting PA from the earliest predeployment stages of any operation. When operationally feasible, commanders should grant media representatives and military personnel supporting PA all possible access to activities without compromising the mission or OPSEC. Develop a command climate and procedures that will allow for full, reasonable access for media representatives.

(5) If requested by ASD(PA), develop and submit proposed PA guidance (PPAG) for approval. PPAG should address PA policy, proposed contingency statements, levels of authority for release or classification of information, declassification guidance, themes, messages and talking points, and responses to anticipated media questions.

(6) Prepare for and assist in the deployment, reception, and operation of the DOD Media Pool. Designate personnel to support the DOD Media Pool when activated.

(7) Establish media operations centers (MOCs), as appropriate, to provide timely public and command information products and services. In coordination with ASD(PA), provide direct PA support, policy guidance, and oversight to subordinate JFCs and their respective MOCs. Be prepared to coordinate US military participation in MOCs established by the responsible multinational force commander and supported by the contributing nations.

The term MOC will be used throughout this publication to represent any type of media support facility (e.g., joint information bureau, combined press information center).

(8) Assist media representatives and military journalists in gaining access to military units and personnel conducting joint and multinational operations, to include commanders, officers, and enlisted personnel directly involved with the military operations. In addition, CCDRs should plan for designated spokespersons to speak with the media regarding the US contribution to the multinational force.

(9) Support other information and imagery requirements as directed.

(10) Plan command information programs to support deployed forces, their home stations, and their family members. Establish ground rules to release information and imagery to civilian media. Information approved for media release should also be provided to the command information staff.

(11) Coordinate and approve resourcing and training for appropriately sized PA organizations in all force packages developed to support joint operations, including civil support (CS) operations as appropriate.

(12) If tasked as a supporting commander, provide PA resources (personnel, equipment, transportation, and communications) to the supported CCDR as identified in approved plans. Be prepared to reinforce the supported CCDR to meet unplanned resource requirements.

(13) Identify COMCAM imagery requirements during operational planning and coordinate with appropriate sources to obtain imagery collection, editing, and transmission requirements and integrate those requirements into COMCAM missions.

(14) Forward imagery that supports joint operations to the Defense Imagery Management Operations Center (DIMOC), DOD's central reception and distribution point for joint interest imagery. Develop procedures to review imagery for security concerns and clear it for public release at the lowest appropriate level.

(15) Employ organic PA capabilities of AC and RC units and individuals mobilized and deployed into an operational area. Provide family members and hometown media with a continuous flow of information to dispel rumors and anxieties, sustain public awareness, and increase understanding of the joint force's missions.

(16) Properly identify individual PA augmentation needs to meet operational requirements.

g. **The Subordinate JFCs:**

(1) Provide overall direction and focus to PA activities in the assigned operational area.

(2) Provide the media and military personnel supporting PA activities access to military operations, to include access to command and staff personnel for briefings and interviews, and appropriate logistics support to accomplish the PA mission.

(3) Designate a joint task force (JTF) PAO and a MOC director, as appropriate.

(4) Select a trained and capable officer to serve as media briefer.

(5) Conduct media interviews when feasible.

(6) Designate an officer to accomplish a security review of VI. VI approved for release should be provided to the MOC as soon as possible for potential release to the media.

(7) Ensure PA participation/coordination in all cross-functional staff organizations.

h. **The Director, Joint Public Affairs Support Element (JPASE).** The JPASE is part of US Joint Forces Command (USJFCOM) Joint Enabling Capability Command. The unit provides joint PA training for the JFC and staff during joint exercises, seminars, and planning events. JPASE has the capability to rapidly deploy in support of geographic CCDRs' PA requirements. The JPASE director has the responsibility to:

(1) Provide JTF PAO if tasked.

(2) Provide or augment JTF PA staff.

(3) Support/conduct forward media operations.

(4) Provide combatant command/JTF PA planning capability.

(5) Provide COMCAM/VI coordination.

See Appendix E, "Joint Public Affairs Support Element," for additional information on JPASE.

i. **The Service Component Commanders:**

(1) Provide a JTF staff PAO and MOC director, if tasked.

(2) Provide media support personnel and equipment.

(3) Coordinate Service component release of information and imagery with higher headquarters PA.

(4) Support the movement of media representatives as feasible.

(5) Assist commercial media otherwise unable to file their products in a timely manner.

(6) Plan for and provide necessary VI documentation teams if tasked.

(7) Conduct command and public information programs per guidance provided by the JFC.

3. **Relationships**

a. **Intelligence.** PA is a customer of intelligence support and uses intelligence products to support PA planning and enhance media analysis, as appropriate. Intelligence requirements are coordinated with the intelligence directorate of a joint staff (J-2). Intelligence's historical and human factors analysis of the adversary gives PA a context from which to understand and anticipate propaganda and disinformation. Additionally, PA may require access to relevant intelligence (including imagery) products to assist in the execution of the PA mission.

b. **Visual Information**

(1) The VI function represents a broad spectrum of imagery products derived from a variety of sources that includes unmanned aerial systems, photo journalists, intelligence assets, weapons systems cameras, and military broadcast organization. PA relies on VI products from many sources to accomplish its mission.

(2) The acquisition of VI by imagery-producing capabilities to support PA must be planned in advance. Imagery requirements need to be synchronized with the operational plans of the imagery-producing capabilities so that imagery captured in support of other mission areas can be exploited by PA.

Additional information on VI CONOPS can be found at http://www.defenseimagery.mil.

c. **Combat Camera**

(1) COMCAM provides VI in support of the JFC's operational and planning requirements.

(2) The deployment of joint COMCAM teams offer a capability to enhance operational and PA missions and JFCs plan for sufficient COMCAM assets. Imagery produced provides operational information for internal and external use. COMCAM teams oftentimes have access to events and areas unavailable to PA, other VI personnel, or media representatives. Furthermore, COMCAM teams have a technological capability for the timely transmission of images during fast-moving operations and the documentation of operations in austere environments.

(3) Because deployed COMCAM teams are usually operationally controlled by the operations directorate of a joint staff (J-3) and support the entire spectrum of an operation, it is essential that the JFC prioritizes PA imagery requirements throughout the planning cycle. Planning includes in-theater declassification and delegation of in-theater release of unclassified COMCAM products to PA to meet time-sensitive media requirements. A COMCAM liaison team is assigned to coordinate imagery requirements and release of imagery products to the media. The COMCAM headquarters management team ensures the timely fulfillment of internal imagery requirements and imagery requests by PA.

For additional details regarding COMCAM policy, procedures, and tasking of COMCAM assets, and appropriate use and distribution of products, see Chairman of the Joint Chiefs of Staff Instruction (CJCSI) 3205.01B, Joint Combat Camera, DODI 5040.04, Joint Combat Camera (COMCAM) Program, and Field Manual (FM) 3-55.12/Marine Corps Reference Publication (MCRP) 3-33.7A/Navy Tactics, Techniques, and Procedures (NTTP) 3-13.12/Air Force Tactics, Techniques, and Procedures Publication (AFTTP) 3-2.41, Multi-Service Tactics, Techniques, and Procedures for Combat Camera Operations.

d. **Information Operations.** PA and IO activities directly support military objectives; counter adversary propaganda, misinformation and disinformation; and deter adversary actions. Although both PA and IO plan and execute public information activities and conduct media analysis, IO may differ with respect to audience, scope, and intent. As such, they are separate functional areas. JFCs ensure appropriate coordination between PA and IO activities consistent with the DOD principles of information, policy, or legal limitation and security.

For additional guidance on the relationship of IO and PA, see JP 3-13, Information Operations.

(1) **Military Information Support Operations.** MISO are used to influence the attitudes, opinions, and behaviors of specific foreign audiences through the dissemination of information. The respective activities of PA and MISO affect each other and require continual coordination.

(a) The PA and MISO planning process should focus on deconflicting activities to avoid countering each other while executing their respective plans to accomplish objectives. Normally MISO and PA activities are coordinated in an IO working group or cell. However, when there is no IO coordination capability, PA and MISO coordinate directly with each other.

(b) Under law, MISO will not be conducted against US persons. However, military information support personnel and equipment may be used to support approved homeland defense or as part of civil authority information support element (CAISE) activities such as information dissemination, printing, reproduction, distribution, and broadcasting. Military information support units in support of CAISE act to inform rather than to influence. All CAISE efforts are coordinated with lead federal agency PA efforts.

For additional guidance on MISO, see JP 3-13.2, Military Information Support Operations.

(2) **Operations Security.** OPSEC measures are designed to identify, control, and protect generally unclassified information that is associated with sensitive operations and activities. OPSEC is concerned with denying "critical information" about friendly forces to the adversary.

(a) PA releases information to the public and must be aware of OPSEC considerations. Security at the source is the primary means of protecting classified and sensitive material and should govern discussions with the public.

(b) PAOs should provide their assessment on the possible effects of media coverage of the joint operation. They should work closely with OPSEC planners to develop guidelines that can be used by military and media personnel to avoid inadvertent disclosure of sensitive information. PA representatives should be involved in OPSEC planning, surveys, and security reviews to protect critical information from public release. A typical OPSEC survey team contains multidisciplined expertise and should include PA.

(c) There is a natural tension between OPSEC and the need to release information and imagery. Decisions as to when to release information and imagery must reflect an understanding of OPSEC. Ground rules allowing temporary transmission delays of potentially sensitive information have proven to be acceptable to the media and effective in balancing short-term security concerns with media coverage requirements.

(d) PA should consider OPSEC issues relating to the use of media and information technology capabilties, such as blogging, cell phones, social networking sites, portable media players, multimedia smart phones, and streaming media.

For additional guidance on OPSEC, see JP 3-13.3, Operations Security.

(3) **Military Deception (MILDEC)**

(a) MILDEC includes actions executed to deliberately mislead adversary decisionmakers as to friendly military capabilities, intentions, and operations, thereby causing the adversary to take specific actions (or inactions) that will contribute to the accomplishment of the friendly mission. MILDEC can be employed during all phases of military operations. Safeguarding MILDEC-related information is critical to the success of the operation; as such, details are classified accordingly.

(b) PA operations should be planned, coordinated, and deconflicted with MILDEC operations consistent with policy, legal limitations, and security. The coordination between PA and MILDEC operations must safeguard the essential elements of deception plans and maintain the integrity, reputation, and credibility of PA as a source of truthful information.

For additional guidance on MILDEC, see JP 3-13.4, Military Deception*.*

(4) **Computer Network Operations (CNO) and Electronic Warfare (EW).** The employment of CNO and EW capabilities can impact aspects of the PA mission. PA and CNO/EW activities should be coordinated to avoid conflicts.

e. **Special Operations.** Special operations forces (SOF) units have assigned PA personnel at the group, regiment, and wing levels, as well as all higher echelons. The SOF PAO advises special operations commanders on the impact their operations are likely to have within the public realm. They ensure the PA policies of higher headquarters are adhered to and balance higher headquarters' need for information and imagery with the sensitive and/or classified nature of their operations. Additionally, the SOF PAO serves as the joint special operations task force (JSOTF) spokesperson and is integrated into all phases of SOF operations. If a SOF PAO is not available, the JFC PAO will assume spokesperson responsibility and will work closely with the JSOTF staff, the theater special operations command PAO and, if needed, US Special Operations Command PA. PPAG referencing SOF operations will normally be provided by the JSOTF PAO. During foreign internal defense and unconventional warfare operations and those missions involving extensive interaction with an indigenous population, the SOF PAO may serve as the link between the command and the senior US DOS representative and/or other designated authority responsible for releasing information to the HN media.

Intentionally Blank

CHAPTER III
PUBLIC AFFAIRS IN JOINT OPERATIONS

"The press is not the enemy and to treat it as such is self-defeating."

Secretary of Defense Robert M. Gates
May 2007

1. Public Affairs Overview

a. **Public Affairs Functions.** PA activities are divided into public information, command information, and community engagement supported by planning and analysis and assessment throughout the course of operations.

(1) **Public information** is information of a military nature, the dissemination of which is consistent with security and the DOD principles of information. While telecommunications technology continues to provide new public information opportunities, military public information is still largely a matter of ensuring media have access to information they need to report on military operations. Media relations activities are designed to provide information to the domestic and international publics. Commanders and their PA staffs should conduct briefings, issue statements, conduct interviews, respond to queries, arrange for access to operational units, and provide appropriate equipment, transportation and communications support to the media. Plans should include specific provisions for each phase of the operation and, as appropriate, the inclusion of media on deploying aircraft, ships, and with deploying units.

(2) **Command information** is communication by a military organization directed to the internal audience to help them understand the goals of the organization, its role in joint operations, as well as significant developments affecting them. Base and organizational publications are traditional ways of reaching these groups. During a joint operation, commanders should consider all dissemination capabilities available, particularly the Internet, to communicate details about the operation and the role of the joint force. When military families are kept informed, affected Service members may be more focused on the mission, particularly when forward deployed.

(3) **Community engagement** is the process of working collaboratively with, and through, groups of people affiliated by geographic proximity or special interest to enhance the understanding and support for military operations. During joint operations, any number of personnel may be involved in activities that engage the community, including but not limited to, PA, civil affairs (CA), MISO, military health specialists, lawyers, and engineers. All community engagement activities should support the overall civil-military operations (CMO) plan. Senior military leaders have responsibilities to engage key leaders in their operational areas, including those from OGAs and nongovernmental organizations (NGOs). PA assists in identifying key leaders and recommending opportunities for military engagement.

b. **Considerations.** The JFC should consider the following in anticipation of conducting joint operations.

(1) **Military operations will draw attention.** Commanders and staffs at all levels must anticipate interest in operations as part of the normal planning process. Unit alerts, increased aircraft activity, and rail or ship loading are highly visible and will almost inevitably lead to media inquiries. Such activities may also cause concern among unit personnel and family members.

(2) **PA should be incorporated in every phase of operations.** Consistent with current DOD PA guidance, and within the constraints of OPSEC, information security (INFOSEC), safety, and privacy of US military personnel, their families, and DOD civilians, PA shall:

(a) Provide accurate and timely information about US military operations and objectives to external (domestic and international) and DOD internal audiences.

(b) Support US and international media coverage of US military operations.

(c) Contribute to global understanding and deterrence by making audiences aware of US resolve, capabilities, and intent.

(d) Mitigate and counter adversary disinformation (propaganda) and misinformation by actively using accurate and timely public information and imagery to preempt and respond to inaccurate information and deception.

(3) **Commanders must evaluate communication activities and associated results.** PAOs should look to all feedback sources to assist in determining the effectiveness of their activities. Results should also be used to inform future plan and strategy development.

2. **Requirements**

a. **General Overview**

(1) PA activities require facilities, personnel, equipment, transportation assets, and communication capabilities. Anticipated PA resource requirements should be identified and addressed as early in the planning process as possible, since PA requirements often exceed available resources. Planning considers specific measures to augment PA personnel and procure, lease, or assign other necessary resources. This generally requires assistance from the supporting combatant commands, Services, and the military departments.

(2) All personnel and equipment should be deployable and provided on a dedicated basis so that the responsible commander can sustain PA operations. Initial PA personnel and equipment should be capable of being carried on both military and commercial aircraft for quick deployment. Follow-on items are given appropriate priority for deployment through logistics channels. The organization and staffing of PA staffs are influenced by the volume and diversity of media assets and the differing nature of their reporting interest. Manning

and operational procedures should also consider the ability of the media to surge for different events at separate locations.

b. **Facilities.** When feasible, facilities with appropriate infrastructure are designated for PA and may include the requirement for establishing and operating a MOC. Specific requirements might include staff and media work areas, equipment storage, imaging facilities, access to helicopter landing zones, and vehicle parking areas. Additionally, work areas are necessary for those personnel conducting the community engagement and command information missions. This includes AFRTS broadcast and transmission facilities. Billeting and messing requirements should also be considered.

c. **Personnel.** The peacetime staffing of most PA offices is likely to be inadequate to respond to the inevitable increase in media and public interest surrounding a crisis. Contingency and crisis action planning (CAP) must address the need for rapid expansion of PA personnel to meet this challenge, especially in the earliest stages of the operation. Augmentation requirements are prioritized and can be filled in the following ways:

(1) **Active Component and Reserve Component PA Units.** Commanders identify the specific skills and capabilities needed to accomplish the PA mission. OPLANs or OPORDs requests for forces (RFFs) should reflect the specific skill sets required. Members of these organizations should train regularly to support these plans and should be provided with sufficient equipment, transportation, and communications support to accomplish the PA functions.

(2) **Individuals.** Service component commanders and supporting CCDRs may also be tasked to support the JFC through the deployment of individual PA personnel. Billets should be identified in advance and individuals matched to specific requirements in support of each operation.

d. **Equipment.** Based on mission requirements, the PAO should identify the equipment necessary to support PA. The planning process should precisely identify the PA infrastructure requirements for each contingency and then identify who will provide them. Maintenance and services essential to sustain the resource packages are also considered.

(1) Every effort should be made to standardize equipment to facilitate interoperability and to minimize additional training requirements, especially in a contingency environment. Specific hardware, software, and digital imaging requirements should be identified to support all PA activities. Considerations include logistic and administrative needs, media and event coordination and scheduling, briefing preparations, and operation of contingency unclassified and classified Internet sites. PA staff, translators, and analysts will generally require TV monitors, video/digital recorders, and reception capability to review newscasts in support of media analysis and assessment.

(2) Deployable AFRTS distribution packages (over air radio/TV broadcast, cable, L-Band downlink), if available, should be considered in the overall requirements. Most of these items must be requested by the CCDR, especially those which support the DOD Media Pool, the command's primary MOC, and other PA offices supporting the operation in its

earliest stages. Broadcast frequencies required should be provided by the communications system directorate of a joint staff. Subsequent resource needs should be met by balanced support provided by the responsible CCDR, the supporting CCDRs, and the Military Departments.

e. **Transportation**

(1) When required, the mobility of the PA effort should match that of other operational forces.

(2) A package of transportation assets, in a combination appropriate to the assigned operation, may include:

(a) Vehicles (with drivers and communications) to support PA administrative and logistics activities.

(b) Vehicles (with drivers and communications) to support the movement of media and PA personnel covering operations.

(c) Force protection assets to travel with PA staffs and media in hostile or unsecured areas.

(d) Aircraft, both fixed- and rotary-wing, to support the movement of media and military journalists.

(e) Surface and air transportation to assist in moving information and imagery products.

f. **Communications.** Specific communications concerns include:

(1) Bandwidth priority to ensure timely (to include near real time or live) transmission of PA and VI products both intertheater and intratheater, to multiple users simultaneously.

(2) Bandwidth allocation for PA products, both classified and unclassified, as files can routinely be more than 250 megabytes in size and during surge events, streaming live at 5 megabytes per second.

(3) Internet access to include unfiltered external access for information and imagery release, local area network access, and establishment and operation of unit and/or contingency unclassified and classified web-based sites.

(4) While communications requirements vary in each situation, an appropriate mix of the capabilities shown in Figure III-1 is needed to support PA.

g. **Other Support.** The PA staff may require certain specialized support based on the type of operation. They should have access to contracting support and a government purchase card in order to obtain goods and services not available within the joint force to

PUBLIC AFFAIRS COMMUNICATIONS REQUIREMENTS

- Telephone lines with international access
- Secure communications
- Mobile radios
- Portable phones
- Answering machines
- Facsimile machines
- Tactical communications devices (secure and nonsecure)

- Live video
- Electronic still photo and video
- Internet access
- Classified and unclassified e-mail accounts
- Dubbing equipment
- Access to satellite uplink equipment

Figure III-1. Public Affairs Communications Requirements

establish and execute PA activities throughout the joint operations area (JOA). This may include:

(1) Contracts for publication of command information products (e.g., newsletters, newspapers, photographs).

(2) Contracts for products, services, and equipment to support media analysis and assessment.

(3) Maintenance and service contracts to ensure sustainability of equipment.

(4) Contracted translation services.

h. **Training and Exercises**

(1) PA personnel and appropriate staff members should be trained in the joint operation planning process (JOPP) and in the tasks involved with joint PA activities. PA training objectives should be included in the command exercise objectives and involve the entire command staff. Prior identification and training of personnel in exercises is essential to their future success in contingency operations.

(2) All aspects of the PA process should be exercised with particular attention paid to coordination with the operational staff, the resourcing of all PA functions, and identifying

and addressing OPSEC concerns. PA universal joint tasks should be used to drive training. Operational scenarios should include events specifically designed to assess the readiness of PA personnel.

3. **Planning**

a. **Overview.** Planning translates strategic guidance and direction into executable OPLANs or OPORDs for contingencies and crisis action responses. Joint operation planning includes all activities that must be accomplished to plan for an anticipated operation—the mobilization, deployment, employment, sustainment, and redeployment of forces. Effective PA planners participate throughout the entire planning process.

b. **Public Affairs and the Planning Process**

(1) The first consideration in PA planning is the commander's intent and desired end state. PA planners consider how desired and undesired effects of PA activities influence the information environment and the accomplishment of the JFC's mission.

(2) PA planners establish and maintain a routine, ongoing relationship with other planners within the combatant command and JTF. Synchronization across the staff facilitates the availability of services and support required to execute PA activities. PA planning should include coordination with the HN, the country team, OGAs, intergovernmental organizations (IGOs), and NGOs, as appropriate.

(3) **Joint Operation Planning Process.** JOPP is a proven analytical process, which provides a methodical approach to planning at any organizational level and at any point before and during joint operations. Examples of specific PA activities taken during JOPP are depicted in Figure III-2.

(a) **Mission Analysis.** PA planners focus on developing situational understanding of the operational environment to include media infrastructure, capability and bias, as well as the social and cultural characteristics of key areas. PA planners analyze the mission, the end state, and objectives, and review applicable strategic guidance to identify the PA tasks (specified, implied, and essential) and develop initial PA staff estimates.

PUBLIC AFFAIRS GUIDANCE

Public affairs guidance (PAG) supports the public discussion of defense issues and operations and serves as a source document when responding to media representatives and the public. PAG also outlines planning guidance for related public affairs responsibilities, functions, activities, and resources. The development and timely dissemination of PAG ensures that all information is in consonance with policy when responding to the information demands of joint operations. PAG also conforms to operations security and the privacy requirements of the members of the joint forces.

Various Sources

JOINT OPERATION PLANNING PROCESS AND PUBLIC AFFAIRS ACTIONS

JOPP Step	Public Affairs Actions

1. Initiation
 	
2. Mission Analysis
	• Begin analysis of the operational environment
	• Participate in JIPOE
	• Review the following for PA implications:
	  ♦ National strategic guidance
	  ♦ SC guidance
	  ♦ Higher headquarters planning directive
	  ♦ Initial JFC intent
	• Provide PA perspective during mission analysis
	• Identify intelligence requirements for PA support to planning
	• Identify specified, implied, and essential PA tasks
	• Develop PA input to the mission statement
	• Conduct initial PA force structure analysis including the need for imagery support, AFRTS, and the DOD Media Pool
	• Develop PA facts and assumptions
	• Develop PA estimates
	• Participate in all cross functional staff organizations related to planning

3. Course of Action (COA) Development 4. COA Analysis and Wargaming 5. COA Comparison 6. COA Approval	• Participate in COA development; identify needed PA capabilities and forces required as well as shortfalls • Participate in COA analysis and wargaming; identify advantages and disadvantages of each COA from a PA perspective • Revise the PA staff estimate as needed based on wargaming • Provide PA input on COA recommendation • Continued participation in all cross functional staff organizations
7. Plan or Order Development	• Refine PA requirements (capabilities, force structure, equipment/logistics, and other resources) to support the COA • Provide PA personnel requirements of the request for forces • Participate in the time-phased force and deployment data build/validation as applicable • Continued participation in all cross functional staff organizations related to planning • Provide input to the operational planning process for all applicable annexes including B, C, D, G, O, V, and draft annex F • Coordinate any administrative or contracting requirements • Develop and submit proposed PAG to higher headquarters for review/approval • Coordinate with subordinate PA staffs to ensure plan synchronization and a smooth transition to deployed operations

LEGEND

AFRTS	American Forces Radio and Television Service	JOA	joint operations area
DOD	Department of Defense	JOPP	joint operation planning process
JFC	joint force commander	PA	public affairs
JIPOE	joint intelligence preparation of the operational environment	PAG	public affairs guidance
		SC	strategic communication

Figure III-2. Joint Operation Planning Process and Public Affairs Actions

(b) **Course of Action (COA) Development.** PA participates in the development, analysis and wargaming, comparison, and approval of COAs.

(c) **Plan or Order Development.** PA planners apply the PA planning considerations in subparagraph 3c, "Public Affairs Planning Considerations," to refine requirements and develop annex F (Public Affairs) of the OPLAN and the PPAG, and support the development of other annexes as appropriate.

<u>1</u>. **Annex F (Public Affairs).** Annex F of an OPORD should address all PA-related transportation, communications, billeting, equipment, and personnel resources required to support the plan. Additional planning considerations that should be captured in the annex are included in Figure III-3. The PA annex to the plan or order complements and supports, but does not replace, the PPAG forwarded to the Office of the Assistant Secretary of Defense (Public Affairs) (OASD[PA]). A sample annex F (Public Affairs) is at Appendix B, "Annex Development."

<u>2</u>. **Annex Y (Strategic Communication).** This SC annex content is spelled out in Chairman of the Joint Chiefs of Staff Manual (CJCSM) 3122.03C, *Joint Operation Planning and Execution System (JOPES) Volume II, Planning Formats.* Content includes the situation and CONOPS focusing on important SC-related elements, such as the overview of the information environment, opposition, lines of operation, measures of effectiveness, tasks, and coordination instructions. PA planners will contribute to the development of annex Y and use the information included to inform the development of annex F.

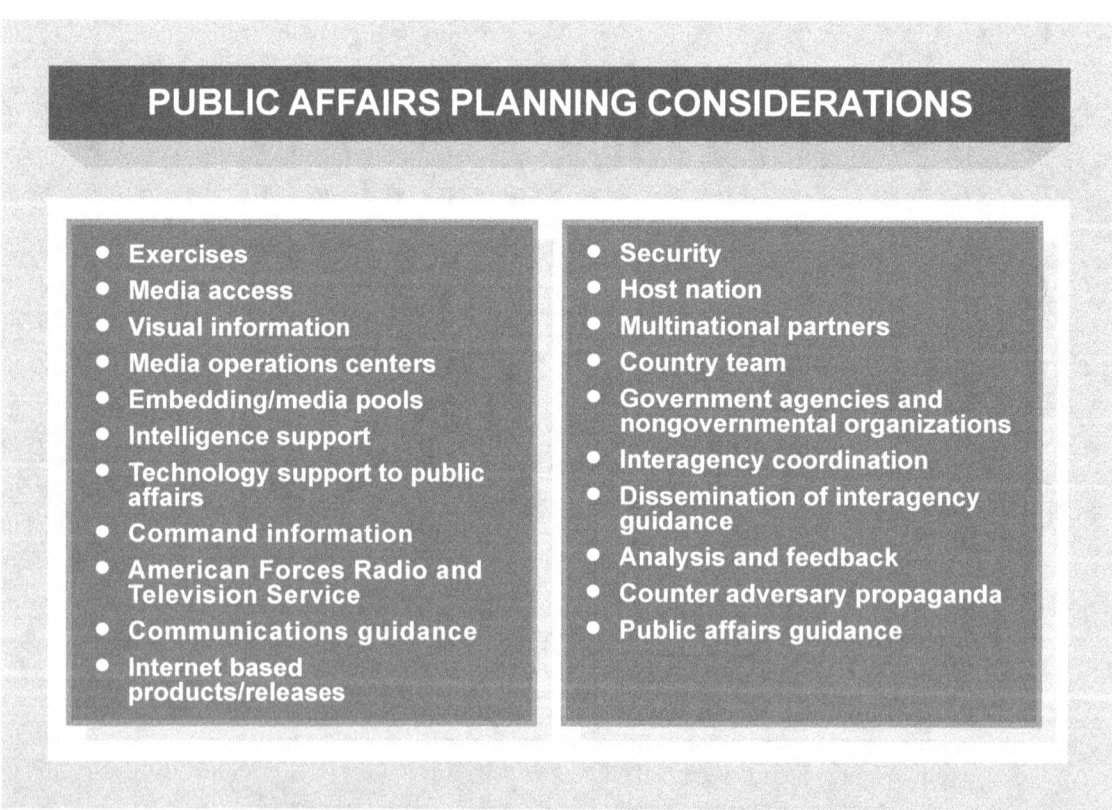

PUBLIC AFFAIRS PLANNING CONSIDERATIONS

- Exercises
- Media access
- Visual information
- Media operations centers
- Embedding/media pools
- Intelligence support
- Technology support to public affairs
- Command information
- American Forces Radio and Television Service
- Communications guidance
- Internet based products/releases

- Security
- Host nation
- Multinational partners
- Country team
- Government agencies and nongovernmental organizations
- Interagency coordination
- Dissemination of interagency guidance
- Analysis and feedback
- Counter adversary propaganda
- Public affairs guidance

Figure III-3. Public Affairs Planning Considerations

3. **Proposed Public Affairs Guidance.** The JFC submits PPAG through CCDRs to OASD(PA) for approval and publication as PAG. PPAG should include recommended PA policy, background, contingency statements, message points, answers to anticipated media questions, community engagement guidance, and details governing the release of information to the public. It should be developed in sufficient time for all required coordination to be complete and initial PAG to be published in conjunction with the receipt of an EXORD. OASD(PA) will staff the PPAG and issue a PAG message approving, approving with modifications, or disapproving the PPAG. PPAG is not used without approval of OASD(PA) or the JFC. At the very latest, approved PAG should be published prior to the start of any deployment activities. Development of additional or supplemental PPAG continues as needed throughout the operation or campaign. The JFC's PA staff recommends additional PA policy, drafts appropriate statements, and identifies any issues and the responses most likely to address the questions, concerns, and interests of external and internal audiences.

4. **Crisis Action Planning.** In CAP, the JOPP steps are time sensitive and often require accelerated decisionmaking to respond to an actual or imminent crisis. In as little as a few days, commanders and staffs must develop and approve a feasible COA, publish the plan or order, prepare forces, ensure sufficient communications systems support, and arrange sustainment for the employment of US military forces. Public and media inquiries may quickly overwhelm organic PA assets and impact PA planning capability. Immediate augmentation of the PA staff may be necessary in order to have the requisite personnel available for planning while simultaneously dealing with increased operational tempo associated with intense public and media interest in the DOD response.

For additional information on joint operation planning, refer to JP 5-0, Joint Operation Planning, *and CJCSM 3122 Series,* The Joint Operation Planning and Execution System.

c. **Public Affairs Planning Considerations**

(1) **Overview.** During initial planning it is critical to synchronize PA planning and activities across the joint force and with other agencies as necessary. Authorities to plan, integrate, approve, and disseminate appropriate information and imagery should be clearly established. Legal considerations regarding release of information on investigations in the JOA, including those regarding alleged law of war violations, should be addressed as early as possible in the PAG. Coordination of overall themes, as well as a plan to support media coverage and all applicable PAG, should be approved prior to hostilities in order to effectively shape the information environment.

(a) As planning continues and preparations for operations begin, the requirement for public information activities increases, as people realize that forces are preparing for a deployment.

(b) With increased public and media interest, the need for PA programs, activities and personnel will continue to expand. PA demands are highest at the outset of operations or outbreak of hostilities. OASD(PA) may embed media and require a MOC and/or subordinate MOCs in geographic areas where operations attract a high concentration of media. Where direct access to operations is not possible, OASD(PA) may require media pools to be established and supported. It is important to continue the synchronization and integration of PA across the staff and with DOD and USG activities (e.g., daily press briefings, response to query, and COMCAM documentation) to counter propaganda.

(c) Many of the same PA activities continue throughout an operation. PA activities should support the return of control to a competent, credible civilian authority, repair of essential information infrastructure, selected augmentation of HN radio/TV/print infrastructure when required to meet the conditions for a transition to civil control or meet end state conditions, and support redeployment activities/coverage.

(2) **Higher Headquarters and Organizational Strategic Communication Goals**

(a) CCDRs develop goals, objectives, strategic estimates, strategies, and plans to accomplish their assigned missions based on strategic guidance and direction, including SC guidance. Similarly, PA planners conduct analysis of strategic direction, SC guidance, and goals to develop their communications strategy and supporting PA plans. SC guidance should be understood by planners from the initial stage of planning and incorporated throughout the process. PA planners should ensure that execution of PA activities not only supports the commanders' operational objectives, but also is aligned with SC guidance. During the planning process, specific intended audiences, themes, messages, actions, desired effects, and objectives should be identified.

(b) Synchronized planning for incorporation of PA, DSPD, IO, and other SC-related capabilities is essential for effective SC. Interagency efforts promote international support from nations in the region and provide an opportunity to advance regional and global partnerships. Therefore, CCDRs should ensure that planning for SC supporting capabilities is consistent with overall USG SC objectives. There also is a mutually supporting relationship between the military's PA and DSPD efforts and similar PA and public diplomacy (PD) activities conducted by US embassies and OGAs.

(3) **Intelligence.** Understanding the operational environment is fundamental to joint operation planning. Intelligence analysts use the joint intelligence preparation of the operational environment (JIPOE) process to analyze, correlate, and fuse information pertaining to all relevant aspects of the operational environment. Developing a systems perspective is one methodology used by intelligence analysts during JIPOE to identify links, nodes, and relationships within and across networks. This could include identification of critical community organizations and individuals that influence the population, media, etc. In order to satisfy information requirements, PA may request that certain platforms conducting surveillance and reconnaissance missions for intelligence purposes also gather imagery to support the PA mission. Accordingly, PA may require access to relevant intelligence products to assist in the development of PA news releases.

See JP 2-0, Joint Intelligence, *JP 2-01,* Joint and National Intelligence Support to Military Operations, *and JP 2-01.3,* Joint Intelligence Preparation of the Operational Environment, *for additional guidance.*

PUBLIC AFFAIRS REQUESTING INTELLIGENCE IMAGERY SUPPORT

During Operation IRAQI FREEDOM, public affairs personnel in the Joint Air Operations Center monitored current operations for the prosecution of sensitive targets. Public affairs planners in the operations center recommended intelligence, surveillance, and reconnaissance platforms gather imagery on sensitive targets to prove coalition aircraft struck the intended military target rather than surrounding civilian buildings and infrastructure. The imagery was declassified for public release.

Various Sources

(4) **Media Operations.** Media want to be at the action. It is essential that commanders understand that members of the press desire to move as close as possible to the action in order to gain a complete understanding of the operation.

(a) PA plans should include detailed processes, procedures, and supporting requirements to give media the opportunity to meet the personnel actively conducting operations. Commanders may embed media with selected units for certain operations or periods of time whenever feasible. This practice enables media to provide much more in-depth reporting by staying with a particular unit or following an operation to its termination. When embedding media, it is essential that specific ground rules be established and that they are thoroughly understood by both the media and the embedded unit. Planning should include detailed provisions for accommodating and supporting the media when deployed with the joint force and escorted by those not formally trained in PA. The commander's security concerns are also addressed when determining what areas the media are allowed to visit.

(b) Commanders also have the option to have media accompany them when they conduct visits to their operating unit in the field. This concept is desirable to media who cannot embed for long periods of time. Media have the opportunity to meet the personnel conducting the operations and have the perspective from senior leaders.

(c) PA should have the capability to support local and regional media consistent with the JFC's instructions and other guidance. Effective public communications requires both cultural and language capabilities. Media facilitation, media response, and media escort operations should be able to accommodate non-English-speaking reporters, especially those of the HN or regional media outlets. News releases and public information Internet sites should have a local/regional language capability. Media analysis must take into account cultural context to provide nuanced evaluation of PA efforts.

(5) **Timely Coverage.** It is critical that plans are developed to assist the media in getting the information out in an accurate and timely manner in order to compete in the information environment. PA plans facilitate the media getting a first-hand look at joint operations. To this end, operational planning should:

(a) Commit equipped and trained joint PA teams.

(b) Determine lift and logistic support to move PA and media personnel and media products to and from forward locations as appropriate.

(c) Hold frequent briefings in theater with international and US media—several per day if needed to keep them apprised of operations as appropriate.

(d) Institute processes for the rapid dissemination of weapons systems video, intelligence, surveillance, and reconnaissance data, and COMCAM products as appropriate.

(e) Delegate the authority for the release of information and imagery to include COMCAM and other related products to the lowest possible level.

(6) **Visual Information and Combat Camera.** When developing and coordinating plans, PA planners work closely with the staff element that has supervisory responsibility for VI and COMCAM operations to ensure PA requirements are identified and taken into consideration. Commercial multimedia products are copyrighted and cannot be used without consent from the copyright holder.

(7) **Command Information.** Commanders should plan for the inclusion of command information personnel in operations. The DOD command information program assists commanders in their leadership communications functions.

(8) **American Forces Radio and Television Service.** The deployment of AFRTS offers the JFC and PAO an important means to communicate directly to DOD personnel in the operational area, as well as DOD personnel and family members in other locations.

> *"During World War II the US Army undertook an aggressive hometown news approach when US troops on the stalemated front in Italy came to believe that they had been forgotten by the folks back home. An aggressive Public Affairs program aimed at telling individual soldiers' stories to their hometown news resulted in a flow of personal mail back to the front, which let the troops know that they were not forgotten."*
>
> **Charles Moskos**
> ***Reporting War When There Is No War***

(a) AFRTS has a wide range of deployable equipment systems, from small unmanned satellite radio and TV decoders used to provide service at small base camps or messing areas to large scale network radio and TV systems. Additionally, AFRTS can provide a MOC with video newsgathering capability for joint command messages.

<u>1</u>. During the initial stages of an operation, AFRTS is one of the timeliest channels to get the CCDR's message to the deployed force.

<u>2</u>. Initial consideration for staffed AFRTS facilities should center on radio service to bare-base and forward areas, with TV considered for rear areas and further

expansion as an operational area matures. PA should anticipate the desire of the DOD leadership to communicate directly to deployed forces.

<u>3</u>. Additionally, AFRTS can be used to transmit immediate announcements to DOD personnel when approved by the CCDR. AFRTS TV capabilities should be considered for installation at messing and recreational facilities and further expanded as the operation develops. A wide range of AFRTS options are available to meet operational requirements.

<u>4</u>. In austere environments, AFRTS is capable of providing a small satellite system to receive radio and TV news coverage, obtain electronic copies of DOD products such as the "Early Bird" and "Stars and Stripes Lite," and other command information releases.

(b) Deployment of AFRTS assets into an operational area usually requires special approvals for frequencies, real estate, and facilities which must normally be coordinated by the MOC. The senior AFRTS officer commands the AFRTS station and serves as a member of the MOC.

(c) AFRTS outlets may not be used for any type of political purpose or MISO and may not produce or broadcast programming to serve interests other than the DOD internal audience.

Refer to Appendix D, "Sources for Defense Media Activity," or contact the DMA (www.dma.mil) for assistance with AFRTS planning.

(9) **Community Engagement.** PA provides specialized skills in planning and developing relationships for commanders seeking to successfully interact within local communities while conducting operations. PA should be involved in the planning, preparation, and execution of engagements within the local/HN communities to support the CMO plan. PA planners should look for creative ways to employ community engagement capabilities.

(10) **Defense Support to Public Diplomacy.** DSPD consists of activities and measures taken by DOD components to support and facilitate USG PD efforts. DSPD ensures that DOD sends a coherent and compelling message in concert with other USG agencies. It is critical that all DOD information activities be conducted in concert with the broader USG communications strategy and support the National Security Strategy. As such DSPD requires coordination across the interagency and among DOD components.

(11) **Country Team.** The country team consists of key members of the US diplomatic mission or embassy and work directly with the HN government. Its purpose is to unify the coordination and implementation of US national policy within each foreign country under direction of the chief of mission (COM). Country teams meet regularly to advise the COM on matters of interest to the United States and review current developments in the country. The COM, as the senior US representative in each HN, controls information release in country. The PA staff should coordinate all themes, messages, and press releases impacting a HN through the respective US embassy channels.

(12) **Interagency Coordination.** CCDRs operate in a public information arena with interagency partners who may not be part of the country team, but whose actions and information can affect public understanding of the facts. Communicating a consistent message that supports approved themes is essential during operations. All participating agencies and organizations need to establish and agree early in the planning process on procedures for media access, issuing and verifying credentials, and briefing, escorting, and transporting media members and their equipment. The Under Secretary of State for Public Diplomacy and Public Affairs plays a key coordinating role in this process. OASD(PA) interfaces with the combatant commands, normally through their joint interagency coordination group, and passes the information down through PAG.

(a) **The Executive Office of the President** is the lead for SC. The DOS's Bureau of International Information Programs engages international audiences on issues of US policy, society, and values to help create an environment that can be receptive to America's national interests. Commanders and their staffs should plan for PA activities to function in coordination with these and other national-level communication initiatives.

(b) **Public Diplomacy.** PD consists of overt international public information activities of the USG designed to promote US foreign policy objectives by seeking to understand, inform, and influence foreign audiences and opinion makers. It is critically important that PA and PD are coordinated in order to ensure consistency of their respective messages and to maintain credibility with their respective audiences.

(c) **Interagency Guidance.** Information from the interagency process, DOD, and various levels of command is disseminated through PAG. This guidance is essential to ensure a consistent message is projected. The guidance can change weekly, daily, or hourly as the political and military situation changes.

(13) **Intergovernmental Organizations and Nongovernmental Organizations.** Close coordination with IGOs and NGOs also can be an important PA responsibility. For example, if DOD is providing foreign humanitarian assistance (FHA), there may be many non-DOD or non-US agencies (e.g., United Nations Office of the High Commissioner for Refugees, the International Committee of the Red Cross) involved. There will be public and media interest in their activities as well as those of DOD. Close coordination by the joint forces with other involved agencies will help ensure consistent information is presented about the total US response effort.

(14) **Host Nation.** PA planners should consult with HN governments as appropriate to identify local issues and concerns that should be reflected in the PAG. This coordination normally is established through the PAO at the respective embassy and in close coordination with IO planners.

(15) **Multinational Partners.** US military forces will rarely work alone to solve an international crisis, thus PA planning should reflect the possibility of multinational partners joining in the effort. In addition to HN sensitivities, the MOC staff should also be cognizant of multinational partners' concerns when communicating with the media and the public.

d. **Public Affairs Planning for Specific Operations**

(1) **Overview.** Commanders should ensure PA activities are tailored to support the joint forces across the range of military operations. While the public and the media are interested in the essential facts of any situation, that information is incomplete without an understanding of the background, underlying rationale, and other fundamental elements particular to a certain type of operation. Experience shows that media interest in civil support, FHA, managing the consequences of incidents, peace operations (PO), and similar operations often peaks early, then diminishes gradually. PA planning should take this into account. Commanders and their PA personnel should be prepared to discuss, among other topics, organizational structure, strategy, objectives, tactics, training, logistics, intelligence, and troop support issues. Explaining the details of such areas reinforces the media and public awareness of how the military functions within the context of the stated political goals.

(2) **Foreign Humanitarian Assistance.** FHA operations are conducted to relieve or reduce the results of natural or man-made disasters. FHA provided by US forces is generally limited in scope and duration. The assistance provided is designed to supplement or complement the efforts of the HN civil authorities or agencies that may have the primary responsibility for providing humanitarian assistance.

(a) These missions involve a delicate balance of political and military objectives. FHA missions include operational and informational coordination with NGO relief organizations. Intense media and public interest in FHA operations may require more than usual PA capabilities. The potential for involvement of multiple USG agencies and IGOs and often the representatives of other involved nations can complicate the coordination required to get approval for the release of information and imagery. JFCs and their PA staffs must exercise care so that, in their attempts to demonstrate DOD responsiveness, concern and assistance do not preempt the authority of the political leadership or HN or appear to be taking credit for successes at the expense of other contributing parties.

(b) If a civil-military operations center (CMOC) is established to coordinate relief efforts, PA will work through the CMOC to coordinate activities. In the absence of a CMOC, PA activities will be coordinated through the JTF staff and with other USG agencies involved via the country team.

See JP 3-29, Foreign Humanitarian Assistance, *for additional guidance.*

(3) **Counterdrug (CD) Operations.** There are a number of specific actions taken to reduce or eliminate illicit drug trafficking that require special attention during planning. Most significantly, there are legal and law enforcement aspects of CD that are extremely sensitive and generate additional concerns in the release of information to the public. Commanders and PA planners must consider the intended and unintended effects of communication when deciding how and when to release information regarding CD operations. The release of information could impact the safety of military personnel, civilian law enforcement officials, and other participants pending judicial cases and the security of intelligence systems and sources. Additionally, DOD most commonly operates in a

supporting role as part of an interagency effort; close coordination with agency PA counterparts is critical to ensure a consistent whole of government PA message. PA plans should account for the appropriate release of information to the public as well as OPSEC measures.

See JP 3-07.4, Joint Counterdrug Operations, *for additional guidance.*

(4) **Combating Terrorism.** Terrorist threats and acts occur in media-intense environments. That, in turn, may make it impossible to prevent coverage that could reveal tactics, techniques, and procedures used in combating terrorism. That means PA planners have to anticipate and make accommodations for the probability of live and near live direct media coverage and strive to provide as much information to the public about DOD activities as possible, consistent with OPSEC, technology security, and INFOSEC. In making information available to the media, PA personnel must balance the legitimate information needs of the public against its value to terrorists. Principal PA objectives of an antiterrorism plan should be to ensure accurate information is provided to the public (including media) and to communicate a calm, measured, and reasoned reaction to the ongoing event. OASD(PA) is the single point of contact for all PA aspects of US military antiterrorism and counterterrorism operations.

For additional guidance on combating terrorism, see JP 3-07.2, Antiterrorism, *and JP 3-26,* Counterterrorism.

(5) **Noncombatant Evacuation Operations (NEOs)**

(a) NEOs are conducted to assist the DOS in evacuating noncombatants, nonessential military personnel, selected HN citizens, and third country nationals whose lives are in danger from locations in a foreign HN to an appropriate safe haven.

(b) The JTF PAO, working with embassy personnel, should plan and coordinate releases concerning the NEO and ensure that the COM or the designated representative has approved all PA announcements. Based on the rapid development of this type of operation, PAOs need to be prepared to conduct media operations in any kind of environment, including afloat (e.g., Lebanon NEO in July 2006).

See JP 3-68, Noncombatant Evacuation Operations, *for additional guidance.*

(6) **Peace Operations.** PO include peacekeeping, peace enforcement, peacemaking, peace building, and conflict prevention efforts. Peacekeeping operations are designed to monitor and facilitate implementation of an agreement and support diplomatic efforts to reach a long-term political settlement. A primary PA concern during PO is that the parties to a dispute may release information that is slanted to support their position. These activities may grow into an orchestrated media operation making it difficult for PA personnel to set the record straight. PA can reduce the level of speculation in the news by providing the media with releasable information on a timely basis.

See JP 3-07.3, Peace Operations, *for additional guidance.*

(7) **Civil-Military Operations and Civil Affairs**

(a) CMO encompass the activities of a commander that establish, maintain, influence, or exploit relations between military forces, governmental and nongovernmental civilian organizations and authorities, and the civilian populace in a friendly, neutral, or hostile operational area. The JFC is responsible for CMO in a joint operation. All CA activities support CMO. By their nature, their missions are normally positive and the results are of interest to the local populace and their media representatives. PA personnel and CA assist in the dissemination of information to local populations. PA personnel have the responsibility to engage the local media and can assist CA with passing information to the appropriate audiences through those media outlets.

(b) PA elements also have the responsibility, through command information outlets, to keep military elements informed of the displaced civilian situation, methods and procedures for their orderly withdrawal from the operational area, and any other information on this issue deemed appropriate by the JFC.

(c) Coordination is required to ensure information released about CMO or CA by PA does not conflict with or complicate the work of the other. Coordination is primarily established through the CMOC, although normal staff coordination takes place through other agencies, such as the IO cell, on a regular basis.

See JP 3-57, Civil-Military Operations, *for additional guidance.*

(8) **Combating Weapons of Mass Destruction**

(a) Combating weapons of mass destruction (CWMD) and chemical, biological, radiological, or nuclear consequence management (CBRN CM) are global missions crossing area of responsibility boundaries, requiring an integrated and synchronized effort, and requiring numerous interagency and multinational partners for effective mission accomplishment. DOD will often be acting in support of another lead agency, or even supporting a multinational effort.

(b) PA should work with USG agencies and NGOs to quickly and effectively communicate risk and response information to the public in order to avoid confusion and hysteria.

(c) The release of weapons of mass destruction (WMD) information may require non-DOD lines of communications and authority such as DOS and other diplomatic points of contact.

(d) Because of their multimedia capabilities, PA assets can often be utilized to support CWMD and CBRN CM missions. If appropriately tasked, units such as COMCAM can provide valuable support for the documentation of WMD sites and CWMD activities.

For additional information, see JP 3-40, Combating Weapons of Mass Destruction; *JP 3-41,* Chemical, Biological, Radiological, and Nuclear Consequence Management; *JP 3-11,*

Operations in Chemical, Biological, Radiological, and Nuclear (CBRN) Environments; *and classified CJCSM 5225.01B*, Classification Guide for Counter Proliferation Information.

e. **Media Access**

(1) There is a need for continuous dialogue between the joint force and the media who are covering its activities. Open and independent reporting are the principal means of coverage of military operations. Commanders should seek regular opportunities to work with the media. Media coverage of potential future military operations can, to a large extent, shape public perception of the joint force and national security environment. Thus, JFCs and their PAOs continually assess their understanding of the direct and indirect effects of potential actions and signals on perceptions, attitudes, and beliefs, and should formulate and deliver timely and culturally attuned messages. This is true for the US public; the public in allied or partner nations, whose opinion have an indirect effect on unity of effort; and publics in countries where the US conducts operations, as well as in adjoining and other regional countries, whose perceptions of the US can affect the cost and duration of our involvement.

(2) PA personnel should act as liaisons but should not interfere with the reporting process. The PA mission includes helping media representatives understand joint force events and occurrences so that media coverage is accurate. The JFC, or a designated representative, should conduct frequent operational briefings to inform internal and external audiences of current military operations and respond to media questions.

f. **Media Credentials and Ground Rules**

(1) The criteria for credentialing journalists are established by the joint force PAO or the MOC director. Credentialing is not intended to be a control measure or means to restrict certain media outlets from access. It is primarily a method of validating individuals as journalists and providing them with information that enhances their ability to report on activities within the operational area. Credentialing media representatives also ensures that, if captured, they are recognized as journalists and treated accordingly under the law of war. Some media will embed with the units for an extended period of time. Embedded reporters will be registered by the joint force and will carry identifying credentials or, as appropriate, Geneva Convention cards.

(2) The MOC serves as a logistic and information base for media relations operations. Journalists seeking credentials from the MOC are asked to agree to ground rules tailored to the specific, ongoing joint operation. Commanders should not provide information to non-credentialed, unregistered journalists without guidance from the joint force PAO or the MOC director.

(3) The CCDR should take reasonable steps to ensure all media representatives have proper credentials in a combat zone, although the increasingly open information environment and the large number of journalists who just "show up" in an operational area make it very unlikely that all journalists will have the proper credentials. Even though journalists not credentialed by DOD may not necessarily be given the same access as those who have credentials, all journalists should still be considered for media pools and should be

strongly encouraged to register with the MOC. During registration, the MOC director should request that non-credentialed journalists abide by the same established media ground rules. Absent unusual circumstances, participating in DOD-hosted training for the media will not be used as a prerequisite for accompanying US forces. The decision to suspend credentials or expel a reporter should only be made with the concurrence of the JFC and the CCDR.

(4) **Ground rules** are developed to protect members of DOD from the release of information that could threaten their security or safety during ongoing operations yet facilitates the media's access to timely, relevant information. Ground rules reconcile the desire of the media to cover military operations with DOD security and safety concerns and are in no way intended to prevent release of derogatory, embarrassing, negative, or non-complimentary information. Media ground rules include requirements designed to protect the security, health, and welfare of the media. For example, media ground rules should include the process for release of information, media access to the commander, and access to the Internet if not commercially available, and the process for unintentional exposure to classified information.

(5) In multinational operations, responsibilities for establishing media ground rules, credentialing media, and, if necessary, expulsion of media, are developed and implemented through appropriate multinational command and staff channels. Media outlets, owned in whole or in part by governments or citizens of rival states, might not receive the same considerations as those working for outlets owned by governments or citizens of friendly nations. However, as in joint operations, non-credentialed journalists may not be given the same access to a combat zone as those who have credentials. They should be encouraged to register at the appropriate information center.

(6) Often the media will not be accompanied by PA personnel. US commanders, with the assistance of PA personnel, should identify shortages of escorts and provide training for non-PA personnel who will serve as escorts. Commanders must develop unit plans tailored to local conditions to accommodate reporters operating under this provision and issue guidance about what information and support they will receive. Appendix C, "Guidelines for Release of Information," contains general guidance on support and information to be provided to media representatives.

g. **Media Pools**

(1) Pools are not to serve as the standard means of covering US military operations. In fact, current communications technology and open media access to most segments of any operational area make media pools more unlikely than in past operations. However, pools may sometimes provide the only feasible means of early access to a military operation. Pools should be as large as possible and be disbanded at the earliest opportunity—within 24 to 36 hours when possible. The arrival of early-access pools does not cancel the principle of independent coverage for journalists already in the area.

(2) Even under conditions of open coverage, pools may be appropriate for specific events, such as those at extremely remote locations, on ships, or where space is limited. In such circumstances, PA plans should specify the number and types of media (including

internal media) who will form the pool. The military determines the size and composition of the pool, usually establishing categories such as, but not limited to, print, broadcast, and trade media to ensure adequate scope and distribution of coverage. The media representatives should determine who fills the spaces in the pool.

(3) The military is responsible for the transportation of pools. To ensure the most complete coverage, commanders should provide dedicated transportation if able. Under conditions of open coverage, JFCs should authorize field commanders to permit journalists to ride on military vehicles and aircraft whenever feasible. Commanders should also follow the guidelines in *The Joint Travel Regulations, Volume 2, Department of Defense Civilian Personnel,* to ensure standardization of policy and procedures.

(4) Consistent with capabilities and the operational conditions, the commander supplies PA personnel with facilities to ensure timely, secure, compatible transmission of pool and independent material. In cases when government facilities are unavailable, media, as always, file by any other means available. As with transportation support, commanders employing media pools are responsible for providing access to communications facilities for news products prepared by the pool. Similar assistance should be provided on a space-available basis for those reporters involved in independent coverage. Commanders should understand the sophisticated communications capabilities available to the media and recognize that early and regular discussions with the media help ensure deconfliction of the electromagnetic spectrum.

(5) Figure III-4 outlines some specific considerations for supporting the DOD Media Pool.

(6) Commanders should realize that the formation of a pool places additional media support requirements on the organization. In those cases in which commanders decide that media pools are necessary, PA planning should include reimbursement from the media depending on location and availability of commercial transportation.

h. **Security Review.** As noted earlier, PA officers should work closely with OPSEC planners to develop guidelines to prevent the inadvertent disclosure of critical information. PA supports OPSEC through strict adherence to established security review programs and other measures to ensure critical information is protected.

4. **Execution**

a. **Overview**

(1) **Organization.** The size and organization of a joint force PA staff varies to accommodate mission requirements. PA organizations have evolved to improve PA support to the JFC in the information environment. The PA staff should be organized and have staff members dedicated to management, plans (future operations and future plans), media operations/MOC, analysis and assessment, command information community engagement, Internet, and administration. Figure III-5 depicts the potential structure of a joint force PA organization.

DEPARTMENT OF DEFENSE MEDIA POOL SUPPORT

- Frequent, comprehensive, unclassified operational briefings for pool personnel.
- Access to areas of ongoing combat or exercise operations. The personal safety of the news media is not a reason for excluding them. The goal is to treat the news media as noncombatants accompanying forces, allowing them to accompany the organizations in the conduct of their missions.
- Reasonable access to key command and staff personnel.
- An officer from the supported command in the grade of O-5 or O-6 to coordinate news media pool requirements.
- Itinerary planning that will enable news media pool members to disperse throughout the operational area.
- Cooperation from all forces participating in the operation or exercise on a not-to-interfere basis.
- Supported command planning for logistic support for pool and escort personnel out of existing contingency or exercise funds. Required support may include, but may not be limited to:
  - Airlift from the continental United States to the operational area or exercise.
  - Theater ground, sea, and air transportation to allow pool coverage of operations.
  - Messing and billeting on a reimbursable basis.
  - Issuance of equipment considered appropriate to the situation (helmets, canteens, flak vests, and cold weather clothing).
  - Access to communications facilities to file stories on a priority basis.

Figure III-4. Department of Defense Media Pool Support

(2) **Location.** The command's PA staff is located with the headquarters element. If an independent MOC is established, it should be at a secure location convenient to the media. Regardless of location, coordination between the joint force PAO and MOC staff is essential.

b. **Public Affairs Management**

(1) The joint force PAO is responsible to the JFC for directing PA activities.

(a) The joint force PAO, with appropriate staff support, is on the commander's personal staff and is directly responsible for all the JFC's PA requirements. The joint force PAO provides PA counsel and support to the commander and provides oversight of all the PA functions and subordinate MOC(s).

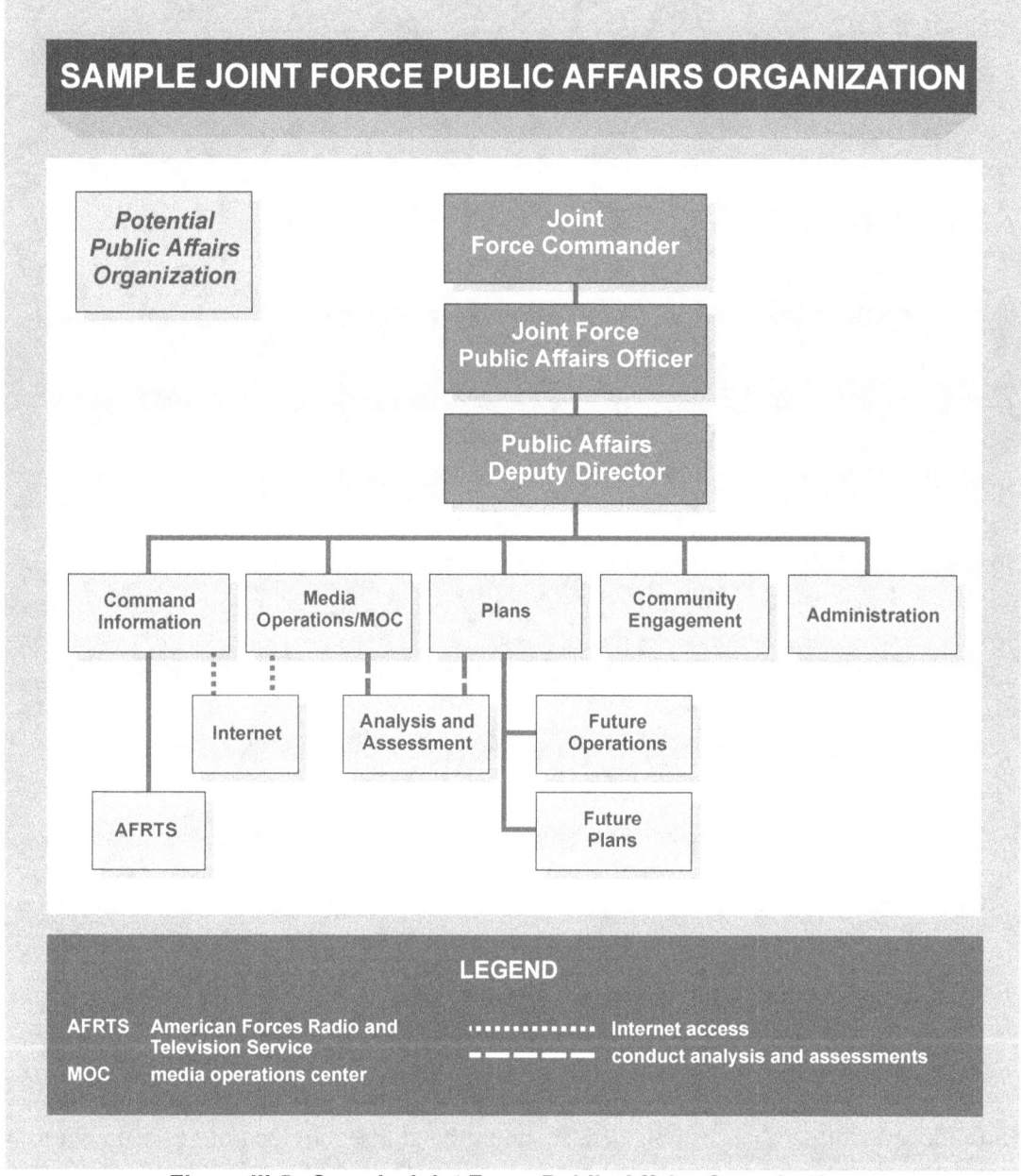

Figure III-5. Sample Joint Force Public Affairs Organization

(b) The MOC director, with supporting MOC staff, is responsible for coordinating all media operations within the operational area, and provides and coordinates support to the JFC through the joint force PAO.

(2) JFCs may opt to have traditional functions of the MOC subsumed under a more robust media operations section, and the joint force PAO may be the sole individual responsible to the JFC for the PA program. Regardless of how the PA staff is organized, typical PA actions or tasks conducted during joint operations are as follows:

(a) Participate in operational analysis, planning, execution, and assessment.

(b) Participate in all applicable cross-functional staff organizations (e.g., boards, centers, cells).

(c) Develop and coordinate communication strategies and guidance.

(d) Prepare PA annexes and support other annex development, as required.

(e) Execute and assess communication strategies and plans.

(f) Evaluate PA resources and provide assessments.

(g) Make recommendations on future PA priorities, near and long term.

(h) Coordinate PA activities with other US agencies, HN, and NGOs as appropriate.

(i) Identify intelligence requirements to support PA planning and assessment.

(j) Identify VI and imagery requirements to the J-3 or designated representative.

(k) Establish and manage a MOC as appropriate.

(l) Monitor/assess public opinion, media coverage, and sentiment analysis.

(m) Modify communication strategies and plans based on assessments.

(n) Plan, coordinate, and assess community engagement activities.

(o) Develop, execute, and assess command information programs.

(p) Provide content for publicly accessible websites.

(q) In accordance with (IAW) with DOD policy, integrate social media into all PA activities.

(r) Provide media training to potential spokespersons.

(s) Disseminate timely, accurate information about military activities.

(t) Respond to media and public inquiries.

(u) Educate JFCs and staffs on the role of information and PA in operations.

c. The **administrative section** provides broad administrative support for the entire PA staff. This section is also responsible for resource support for the PA staff and monitors the status of manning levels and readiness. Additionally, this section may contract for cultural or linguistic assistance as required.

d. **Plans.** PA planners support future operations and future planning, and they coordinate PA planning throughout the JOA. They participate in all applicable boards, bureaus, centers, cells, and working groups, and convert strategic guidance into PA plans for future OPORDs, fragmentary orders, and future plans.

e. **Community Engagement.** This section is responsible for providing PA planning and execution support for activities that promote the interaction of US forces, multinational partners, and HN populations throughout the JOA. It requires close coordination with the country team and HN as well as the CMOC and IO cell/planners to identify community engagement opportunities for the JFC and key staff.

f. **Analysis and Assessment.** This section supports both plans and media operations/MOC. They represent PA in all assessment-related cross-functional organizations and work with the J-2 staff to identify PA assessment requirements and support PA current operations and plans sections with assessment products. For additional information on assessment, see paragraph 5, "Assessment."

g. **Media Operations Center.** Media operations may be the sole purview of a MOC or conducted by a media operations section; the requirements remain basically the same.

(1) A MOC is the central point of contact between the military and media representatives covering operations. It offers a venue for commanders and PA staffs to discuss their units and their roles in the joint operation and helps journalists obtain information quickly and efficiently on a wide variety of complex activities. It should be staffed to support local and regional non-English speaking media. It may also support command information activities. The early establishment of MOCs is an important step in the responsive and efficient facilitation of media operations.

(2) The size and specific structure of a MOC may vary depending on the mission. A sample organizational structure of a MOC is shown in Figure III-6. The functions listed below are common to all MOCs and require appropriate planning and resourcing to effectively support the media relations mission. In small MOCs, each assigned staff member may be responsible for more than one function.

(3) **The MOC director** is responsible for all activities conducted by the MOC staff. This includes close coordination with the J-2, J-3, and foreign disclosure officer to ensure that releasable information is accurate, timely, and issued within current OPSEC guidelines. The MOC director also considers HN sensitivities and media guidelines. The MOC director should develop an appropriate mix of activities to provide maximum opportunity for the media to cover operations directly when possible and practicable as well as acquire and disseminate releasable information and imagery about the conduct of operations and the forces executing the mission. The MOC should also provide materials to the Services' hometown news centers and Services' PA offices. Potential MOC tasks include:

(a) Credential media.

(b) Maintain a media database.

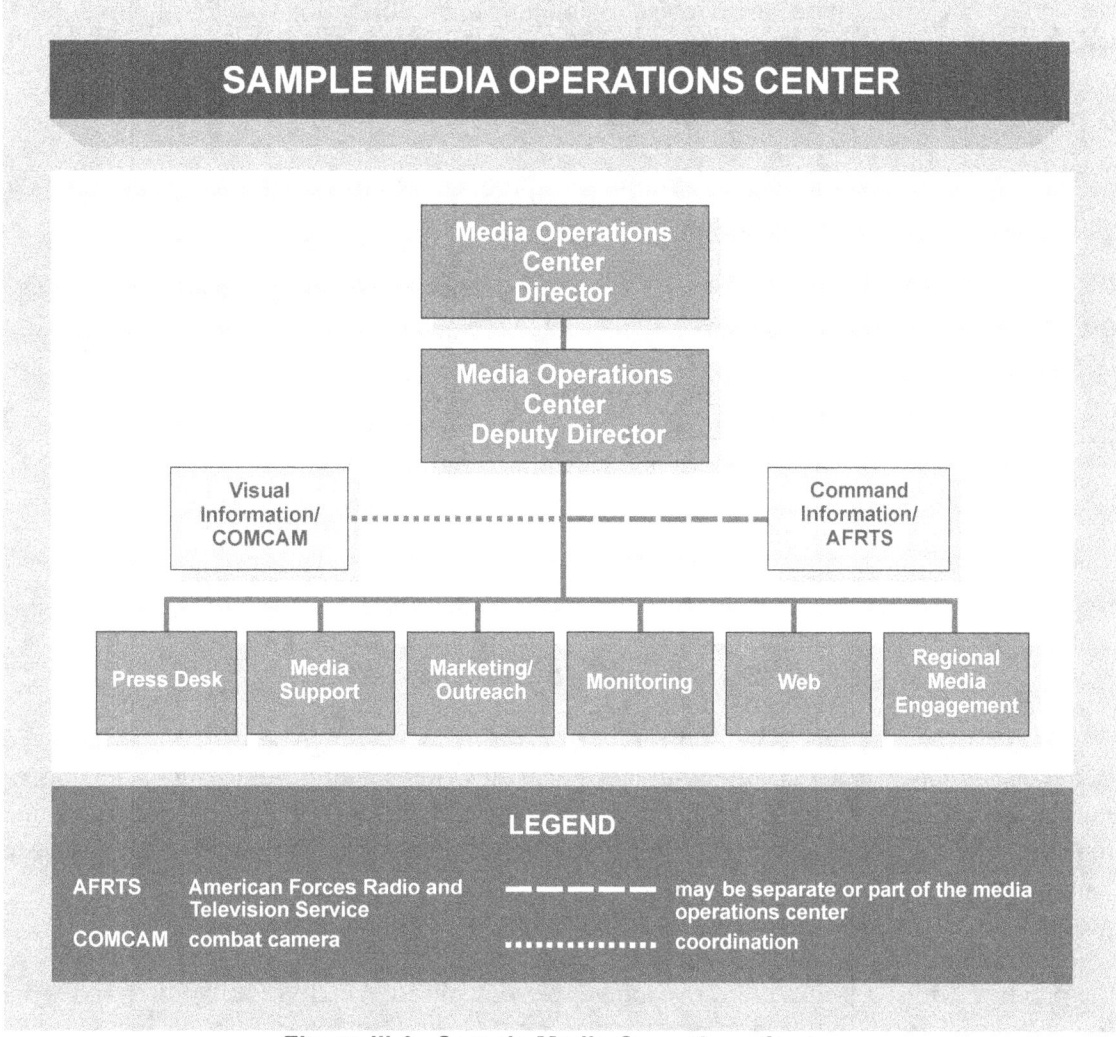

Figure III-6. Sample Media Operations Center

(c) Coordinate media embeds.

(d) Identify logistic requirements.

(e) Obtain/provide vehicles (armored as required) and escorts (armed as required) in order to move media to cover events.

(f) Provide necessary force protection gear to media representatives.

(g) Coordinate subordinate unit PA coverage of critical events.

(h) Coordinate the acquisition and transmission of imagery, information, and interviews to support the PA strategy.

(i) Coordinate requirements for VI support (including COMCAM) with appropriate staff.

(j) Facilitate the review of all imagery and information OPSEC and INFOSEC issues.

(k) Edit as necessary and post content to the publicly accessible website(s).

(l) Cover military operations and produce information packets, news releases, and stories for distribution to external and internal audiences.

(m) Translate all releases and disseminate in the major languages indigenous to the people in the operational area and other intended audiences.

(n) Coordinate interview requests.

(o) Coordinate briefings for local and regional media.

(p) Coordinate briefings from the operational area with US media.

(q) Receive, respond, and track media queries.

(r) Support command information activities.

(4) **The deputy MOC director** assists in the management of the MOC and performs the functions of the director when necessary. Responsibilities include oversight of military-media communications, assessment of available published media products, and liaison with the joint force operations staff and subordinate commands to ensure a continuous flow of timely information.

(5) Personnel working the **press desk** interact directly with the media and serve as the primary point of information exchange. Responsibilities include responding to media inquiries, preparing and issuing news releases, arranging for interviews, and conducting briefings. Additional tasks involve preparing joint force operational briefers, assisting senior commanders in their encounters with the media, supervising/integrating activities of the media support and HN engagement team sections. This section may include representatives from non-DOD agencies, NGOs, and the HN directly involved with the operation to facilitate coordination of publicly released information among all key players. Additionally, there may be a requirement to send press desk personnel as liaisons to these organizations to ensure a timely, efficient, and accurate exchange of information. In multinational operations PA personnel from other countries may work in the press desk section to represent their nation's interests with the media.

(6) The **media support section** is responsible for helping the media cover joint force activities. Specific tasks include coordinating/managing transportation, communications, and logistic support; credentialing media; and supporting media pools. In cases where escorts are required, this section matches the media with knowledgeable persons to facilitate their movement around the operational area. If a security review is required, the media support section ensures that it is done efficiently.

ESCORTS

It is mutually beneficial to both the joint force commander and the media to have escorts available to assist the reporters as they move about the operational area. These escorts need not be trained public affairs personnel, but should be knowledgeable members of the visited organizations who have received training in media relations. These individuals support the joint force by serving as facilitators to assist the media. They should neither interfere with the process of reporting nor attempt to inhibit military personnel from talking about their jobs or missions consistent with security and operational restrictions.

Various Sources

(7) The **marketing/outreach** section is responsible for conducting liaison with media outside the JOA to determine interest in ongoing operations and repurpose existing PA products (video, audio, still imagery, print, and web) or arrange for new PA products to support their needs as well as coordinating remote interviews with commanders and subject matter experts. This section also coordinates holiday greetings and special events programming. Additionally, they produce opinion pieces, speeches, and presentations to support outreach efforts and coordinate speakers for organizations in the United States.

(8) **New Media**

(a) **Public Website.** Using the Internet provides the JFC with a powerful tool to convey information quickly and efficiently on the nature and scope of the JFC's mission, put operational actions into context, and counter adversary propaganda supporting both public and command information activities. This section is responsible for the management and content maintenance of the site.

(b) **Interactive Internet Activities.** JFCs may allow the use of interactive Internet activities (email, blogs, chat rooms, and social media) to support operations. Such use will be IAW current DOD guidance. Under the scope of such an effort, unless otherwise approved, only PA personnel engage in interactive Internet activities with journalists employed by media organizations or with individuals and websites that may be considered equivalent to an established news organization. Additionally such activities should be conducted in the language and idiom of the intended audience, and special attention should be given to use only culturally appropriate messages and materials.

(9) **Monitoring Section.** This section is responsible for monitoring electronic and print media. They develop and distribute summaries and transcripts of media coverage, press conferences, and other significant events.

(10) **Regional Media Engagement.** The section is responsible for establishing and maintaining relations between the joint force and the local and regional non-English media. They facilitate media events with and distribute press releases to local and

regional media as well as monitor and translate their coverage. This section is staffed with linguists as required to conduct translations.

(11) **Command Information.** While command information is primarily a Service responsibility, a properly manned MOC should include staffing to support this vital mission.

(a) At a minimum, the MOC director should ensure internal media are treated fairly and equally with external media and allotted an appropriate share of limited resources such as PA seats on military transportation. Further, commanders should provide all external news releases, along with any responses to query, to command information channels.

(b) AFRTS is resourced to supplement the PA's command information mission and will generally be a division within the MOC working for the MOC director. MOCs employ AFRTS capabilities, including use of the Internet and use of print products to convey joint command messages not only to the deployed force, but also to the home station and to family members. The MOC director ensures the information provided through external and internal channels is coordinated and consistent.

(12) **COMCAM.** While PA usually has organic imagery acquisition capability, it may require imagery from other VI capabilities. COMCAM is a principle provider of VI and generally receives operational tasking from the J-3. PA should identify and coordinate imagery requirements that exceed organic capabilities with the J-3 staff member in charge of tasking COMCAM. Additionally, all COMCAM imagery should be available to PA for review and possible use consistent with OPSEC and INFOSEC.

(13) **Sub-MOCs.** The PAO may recommend the establishment of sub-MOCs based on the size of the operational area, the dispersion of the joint forces, the diversity of Service components, and the variety of concurrent missions. Normally smaller than the main MOC, a sub-MOC should perform the same functions assigned to any information bureau. A sub-MOC may be set up temporarily to support a specific mission or at an established location to assist covering a particular sector of the operational area. Sub-MOCs could also be established afloat to support maritime aspects of a joint operation.

5. **Assessment**

a. Assessment is a process that measures progress of the joint force toward mission accomplishment. It occurs at all levels and across the range of military operations. Continuous assessment helps the JFC and joint force component adjust operations to ensure objectives are met and the military end state is achieved. The primary emphasis of the PA assessment is identifying, measuring, and evaluating implications within the operational environment that the commander does not control, but can influence through a coherent, comprehensive communications strategy established by early integration in the planning process.

CRITERIA USED IN IRAQ

Criteria that formed the basis for assessment used by Multi-National Force-Iraq for strategic communication activities to determine alignment among facts on the ground, media framing of events, and Iraqi perceptions are provided as follows:

- Understanding of the Iraqi and Pan-Arab media.
- Media penetration of key themes.
- Alignment of key messages.
- Understanding Iraqi perceptions.
- Prevalence of misinformation and disinformation in media stories.
- Resonance of press conferences and key themes and messages.

Operation Iraqi Freedom Strategic Communication
Analysis and Assessment
Thomas M. Cioppa
Media, War, and Conflict, April 2009, Vol. 2, pp. 25-45

b. The assessment process begins during mission analysis when the commander and staff consider what to measure and how to measure it to determine progress toward accomplishing a task, creating an effect, or achieving objectives. To enable assessment during execution, baselines for what is going to be measured should be established at this point.

(1) PA planners should determine objectives for PA activities that support achievement of the JFC's strategy as well as relevant assessment measures and criteria to determine success. The PA staff collaborates with members of the joint force staff on assessment development.

(2) This initial set of criteria becomes the basis for future assessment.

c. PA assessments require monitoring, measuring, and analyzing relevant information (media coverage, Internet content, polls, intelligence products, etc.) to evaluate the success of PA activities. During execution, assessments drive adjustments to both current operations and future planning to improve effectiveness. In addition to modifying activities, assessments may identify a requirement to revalidate PA resources and modify them accordingly.

Intentionally Blank

CHAPTER IV
JOINT PUBLIC AFFAIRS IN DOMESTIC OPERATIONS

"…Without timely, accurate information or the ability to communicate, public affairs officers at all levels could not provide updates to the media and to the public…. Federal, State, and local officials gave contradictory messages to the public, creating confusion and feeding the perception that government sources lacked credibility."

The Federal Response to Hurricane Katrina: Lessons Learned

1. Overview

a. The conduct of PA in domestic operations (within the US and its territories and possessions) is somewhat different for DOD in terms of planning and execution; however, unless addressed specifically in this chapter, doctrine for non-domestic joint operations applies.

b. Per Homeland Security Presidential Directive-5, DOD PA operates in accordance with guidance in the National Response Framework (NRF) incident communications emergency policy and procedures (ICEPP), which provides detailed guidance to all federal incident communicators during a federal response to an event. It establishes mechanisms to prepare and deliver coordinated and sustained messages, and provides for prompt federal acknowledgement of an incident and communication of emergency information to the public. The ICEPP is comprised of two annexes contained in the NRF:

(1) **PA Support Annex.** Describes the interagency policies and procedures for incident communications with the public.

(2) **Emergency Support Function (ESF) #15—External Affairs Annex with Standing Operating Procedures.** Outlines the functions, resources, and capabilities for external affairs including PA.

c. Under the NRF, the Department of Homeland Security (DHS) retains the lead for federal public communications and is responsible for activation of ESF #15. DOD typically acts as a supporting agency to a primary or coordinating agency.

d. Federal assistance, including assistance from DOD, can be provided to state, tribal, and local jurisdictions, and to other federal departments and agencies, in a number of different ways through various mechanisms and authorities. Often, federal assistance does not require coordination by DHS and can be provided without a Presidential major disaster or emergency declaration. Examples of these types of federal assistance include that described in the National Oil and Hazardous Substances Pollution Contingency Plan, the Mass Migration Emergency Plan, the National Search and Rescue Plan, and the National Maritime Security Plan. These and other supplemental agency or interagency plans, compacts, and agreements may be implemented concurrently with the framework, but are subordinated to its overarching coordinating structures, processes, and protocols.

For further information on CS, see JP 3-28, Civil Support, *and JP 3-27,* Homeland Defense.

2. Requirements

a. **Personnel.** PA and VI personnel requirements for domestic operations vary based on the situation. There are existing joint OPLANs and joint manning documents that specify the personnel requirements for certain potential operations. Additionally, the CJCS issues a standing defense support of civil authorities (DSCA) EXORD annually that allows force providers to consider potential requirements and place needed personnel in a prepare to deploy order status.

b. **Facilities.** Normally, PA operations are conducted in fixed buildings (hotels, armories, office buildings, etc.) when supporting domestic operations. In many situations, commercial telephone and Internet connections (wired, wireless, and cellular) will be available. In the case of state funerals or other planned operations, the facilities may be pre-designated and wired to support PA. Personnel supporting PA operations will generally use commercial lodging and local restaurants.

c. **Equipment.** When required, PA and VI personnel, who deploy in support of domestic operations, should have a cellular phone and a laptop computer with wireless access or an aircard. PA personnel with access to portable broadcast quality imagery transmission systems should be prepared to deploy with and support operations with those systems. PA and VI personnel should deploy with digital cameras and have still and motion imagery editing and data transfer software on their laptops. Note: Personnel will not always have access to the ".mil" domain during domestic operations.

d. **Training.** All PA and VI personnel ordered to deploy in support of domestic operations should have working knowledge of the NRF as it pertains to PA. Online Federal Emergency Management Agency (FEMA) training courses are available at http://training.fema.gov.

3. Planning

a. PA planning for domestic operations essentially follows the same phases as for other joint operations. PA plans for DSCA are tailored to support the ESF #15 requirement to provide accurate, coordinated, timely, and accessible information to affected audiences, including governments, media, the private sector, and the local populace, including the special needs population. It is critical that PA activities are planned, coordinated, and integrated across jurisdictions, agencies, and organizations both government and private.

b. PA planners ensure that plans and associated annexes delineate responsibilities, processes, and logistics as appropriate in support of ESF #15 as follows:

(1) Coordination of messages with federal, state, tribal, and local governments.

(2) Support for the MOC.

(3) Gathering information on the incident.

(4) Providing incident-related information and imagery through the media and other sources in accessible formats and multiple languages (as necessary) to individuals, households, businesses, and industries directly or indirectly affected by the incident.

(5) Monitoring news coverage to ensure that accurate information is disseminated.

(6) Handling appropriate special projects such as news conferences and press operations for incident area tours by government officials and other dignitaries.

(7) Providing basic services, such as communications and supplies, to assist the news media in disseminating information to the public.

c. Exercises are a key element for successful domestic operations and support the planning effort. PA and VI personnel participate in exercises and conduct objective assessments of capabilities so that issues are identified and remedied prior to a real incident.

(1) **Exercise Planning.** Exercise planning provides an exceptional opportunity to inform other agencies about DOD PA roles, responsibilities, and capabilities. Interagency PA working groups should be integrated into the joint exercise lifecycle process. These groups should include PA and VI participants from DOD as well as participating federal, state, tribal, and local agencies. Note: Planners need to be aware that there will be both a significant "real-world" and "simulated media" requirement which must be supported.

(2) **Exercise Execution.** During exercises, DOD PA and VI participants have the opportunity to perform PA operations in the exercise's scenario being simulated, participate in dissemination of real-world information to exercise participants, and practice with other agencies during events that can draw significant media and public attention.

4. Execution

a. Domestic situations which require a military response are generally short or no notice events. Specific DOD PA responsibilities are outlined in various combatant command plans and standing PAG. The EXORD for the incident will provide the PA posture and media engagement policy. Incident specific guidance will be developed by the primary agency in coordination with participating agencies.

b. Domestic operations are planned and executed in three phases, consistent with the DHS operations. DOD PA support evolves as follows:

(1) **Shaping.** The DOD is rarely a "first responder" for domestic situations. In this phase PA manages expectations regarding DOD's response among both the public and the other responding agencies. PA activities include developing themes and messages that clearly explain the scope and timing of the DOD response.

(2) **Engagement.** This is the phase where military forces are actually on-scene supporting an incident and PA is actively informing the public about DOD activities via releases of information and imagery, press conferences, and site visits.

(3) **Transition.** This is the phase where military forces begin to disengage from incident response support. It is critical that PA activities in this phase articulate why DOD support is no longer required.

c. Initial DOD PA involvement in DSCA will be through the defense coordinating officer (DCO) assigned to the applicable DHS/FEMA region involved and the defense coordinating element (DCE) if established. The DCO and the DCE process requirements for military support, forward mission assignments to the appropriate military organizations through DOD-designated channels, and assign military liaisons, as appropriate, to activated ESFs.

(1) PA personnel provide initial assessments of situation to the DCO, DCE, and combatant command PA staff in terms of requirements for personnel and equipment. They provide initial interface with other deployed federal public information officers (PIOs), and serve as the DOD liaison for the media.

(2) As the DOD response grows, PA personnel deploy with the operational command post or joint force lead element to coordinate DOD PA activities and involvement in the incident.

(3) Other units tasked to deploy in support of domestic operations should also include a PA element in their headquarters staff. This PA element should be prepared to actively engage the media to show how the unit is supporting the federal response.

d. **Joint Information Center.** A substantial portion of the overall PA effort will be supporting the media to ensure affected populations are receiving necessary information. In order to coordinate the timely release of emergency/incident-related information, imagery, and other PA functions, a joint information center (JIC) may be established (see Figure IV-1).

(1) The JIC is normally located close to the best sources of information about the situation, such as an incident command post or emergency operations center. Note that DOD and other agencies will often have a separate staff performing PA duties/functions on behalf of their own agency. In the absence of a JIC, coordination still needs to occur between DOD, other agencies, and the primary agency.

(2) When a JIC is established, the responsible commander ensures that adequate PA personnel are assigned whenever DOD forces deploy. However, the bulk of DOD PA personnel supporting the incident will be assigned to the JFC.

(3) A JIC is most useful when multiple agencies and organizations come together to respond to an emergency or manage an event and need to provide coordinated, timely, accurate information to the public and other stakeholders. Under the Incident Command

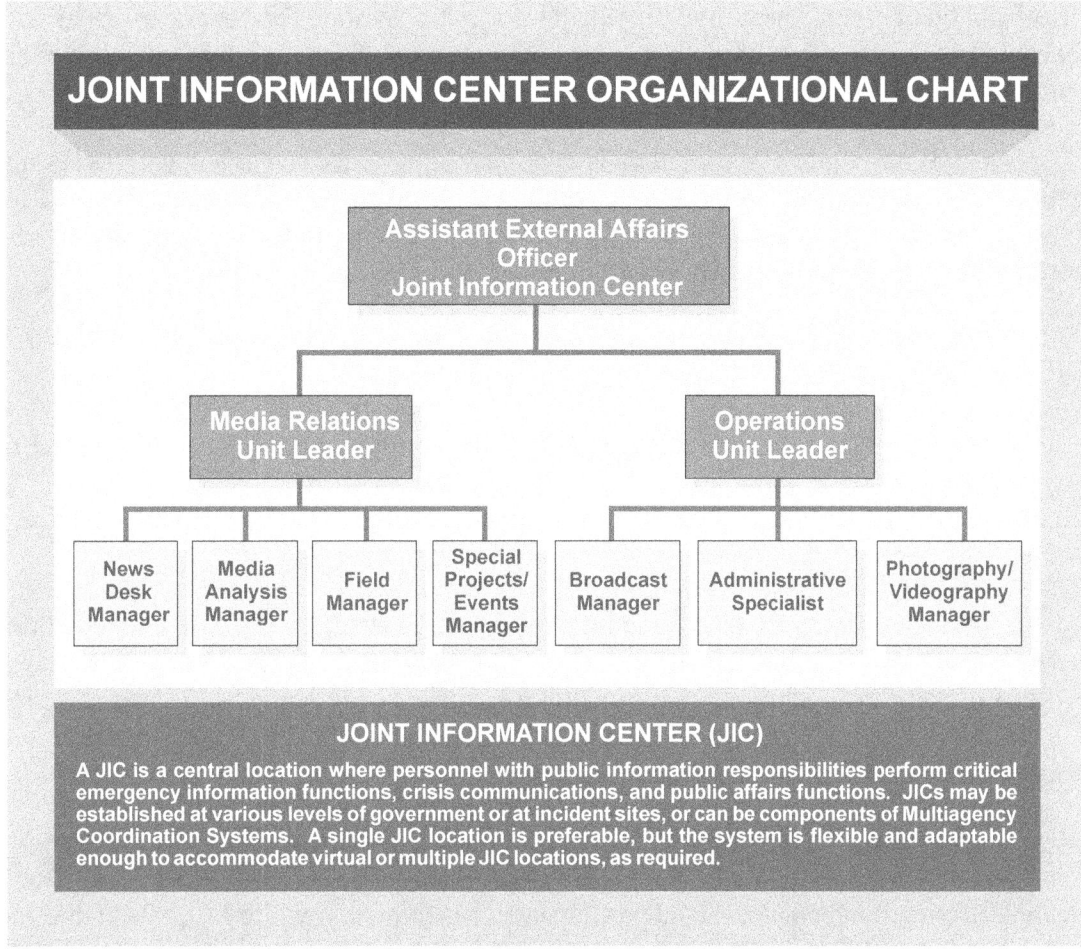

Figure IV-1. Joint Information Center Organizational Chart

System, the PIO is one of the key staff supporting the command structure. The JIC carries out the PIO's responsibilities and has three primary responsibilities:

(a) Gather incident data.

(b) Analyze public perceptions of the response.

(c) Inform the public and serve as the source of accurate and comprehensive information about the incident and the response to a specific set of audiences.

For detailed guidance on JIC structure and function, refer to The National Response Team Joint Information Center Model.

(4) DOD PA releases its own information and imagery, and conducts media operations, but the products should be coordinated with either the primary agency or the JIC to ensure consistent messages and avoid the release of conflicting or incident-sensitive information.

e. During DSCA, combatant command PA personnel monitor the **National Incident Communications Conference Line (NICCL)** that is used for transmission and exchange of critical and timely (e.g., "breaking") incident information among federal and affected state, local, and tribal authorities. It is a key source of emerging information for PA activities and communications synchronization.

(1) If the nature of the incident is of critical importance and urgency, DHS PA may continuously monitor the NICCL to receive updates from departments and agencies. The DHS PA staff will maintain a summary of key NICCL communications and interagency coordination actions to inform DOD and other agencies' PA activities.

(2) DOD and combatant command PAO will receive DHS issued incident PAG and daily summaries via the NICCL when ESF #15 is activated.

(3) During sustained incident management activity, the NICCL will be used for daily or other incident communications coordination calls. The combatant command PAO will maintain and distribute NICCL information to subordinate PA participants in a timely manner.

(4) There are more than 80 federal interagency partners, 54 states and territories, the District of Columbia, 562 tribal entities, and thousands of local governments that may be involved in domestic operations. This creates a significant challenge for PA coordination. The NICCL and state incident communication coordination lines are invaluable for coordinating PA efforts.

f. **DOD Public Affairs Guidance.** The OASD(PA) will develop PAG for domestic operations that is consistent with that of other operations and DHS PAG, but also includes relevant information from non-DOD participants. Additionally, while DOD PAG does not apply to other agencies, it should be coordinated with and distributed to all participating organizations. The PAO may produce a PA strategy document where PAG is not appropriate or feasible.

g. **Command Information.** Based on the ubiquitous nature of the media and multiple channels of communication, command information requirements are not significant in domestic operations. However, in extended domestic operations, it may take on a larger role.

5. Assessment

As with all military operations, on-going assessment of public communication activities by DOD PA personnel is critical to support follow-on planning as well as inform future operations. How the USG responds to domestic situations will be of interest to other countries and covered by their media. PAOs and PA staffs conduct analysis of international coverage of DOD activities to assess the character of their reporting as well.

NOTIONAL DOMESTIC RESPONSE

When a no-notice incident occurs, the local jurisdiction handles the initial response including public information and may establish a joint information center (JIC) to integrate the public communications efforts of local agencies. If the Department of Defense (DOD) is involved at this point, a military public affairs officer (PAO) should participate in the local JIC.

When a Federal response is required, usually the first integrated public affairs (PA) action is for the Department of Homeland Security to conduct a National Incident Communications Conference Line (NICCL) call. During this call, the initial integrated public affairs guidance (PAG) is crafted where control (lead agency for public communications effort), coordination (how supporting agencies will coordinate public communication), and communication (key messages) are addressed. The supported combatant commander's PAO and Office of the Secretary of Defense PAO should be participants in the call. The combatant command promulgates resulting guidance to responding DOD forces.

As the event evolves, emergency support function #15 and a JIC for federal responders is established. This JIC may be integrated with the local JIC or become a stand alone center. All participating Federal agencies provide representatives to this JIC to represent their agency and serve as the JIC staff. The combatant command PAO recommends PA personnel for the JIC. Personnel assigned to the JIC will perform tasks assigned by the JIC manager.

As military forces arrive at the incident, the joint task force (or similar headquarters element) will establish a PA function primarily to perform significant media support operations. Based upon the PAG, DOD PA personnel will facilitate media access and coverage of the DOD activities. DOD PA efforts will be coordinated with other agencies through subsequent NICCL calls and through the JIC.

The JIC will usually produce products dealing with the overall federal response and coordinate and conduct joint press conferences at or near the incident site. DOD efforts at the incident will be coordinated with the JIC so that federal communication efforts are consistent and mutually supportive. DOD will often participate in or provide subject matter expert support to joint media events.

Note: The term "joint" when used in JIC, refers to "multi-agency."

SOURCE: US Northern Command Joint Public Affairs Support Element

Intentionally Blank

APPENDIX A
COMMANDER'S COMMUNICATIONS STRATEGY

1. Overview

a. Successful military communication that supports the achievement of joint force objectives as well as those up to and including that of the USG requires carefully coordinated and synchronized communication strategies. At the operational level, the ability for the military commander to promulgate information informing and influencing selected audiences is a critical element to successful operations. Commanders who develop and execute communication strategies derived from and aligned with SC themes and messages increase the opportunity for success.

b. The commander's communications strategy should be an element of the commander's larger overall strategy and is supported by the broader SC effort. An effective communications strategy is commander driven, proactive, and ensures that the potential results of tactical actions on the information environment are considered and addressed prior to execution. While any action taken by the joint force may influence the information environment, PA, IO, and DSPD activities are planned specifically to shape it. Communications strategy facilitates coordinated communication efforts focused on reaching individual audiences via the most credible and effective means available.

2. Strategy Development

a. Developing a comprehensive communications strategy requires an integrated process that synthesizes all means of communications and information delivery. In addition to synchronizing the communication activities within the joint force, an effective communications strategy is developed in concert with OGAs as well as multinational partners and NGOs as appropriate. Additionally, commanders should be cognizant of the impact that joint force communications activities have on the other three instruments of national power (diplomatic, informational, and economic) as well as their implications for the total operational environment including political, military, economic, social, information, and infrastructure systems.

b. Initial planning guidance sources used to develop the communications strategy include the overall USG strategy and SC guidance, SecDef and Joint Chiefs of Staff guidance as well as the associated combatant command regional strategy and the joint force mission. Within the joint force, communications strategy planners use the theater campaign plan, operation plan, commander's planning guidance, and desired outcomes to shape their work across the current operations, future operations, and future plans horizons.

c. Communications strategy development is often accomplished in a cross-functional working group as depicted in Figure A-1. Input from key functional staff members informed by information from various levels above and below the joint force headquarters as well as assessment of past activities helps communication planners refine future efforts and messages to better meet stated communication objectives.

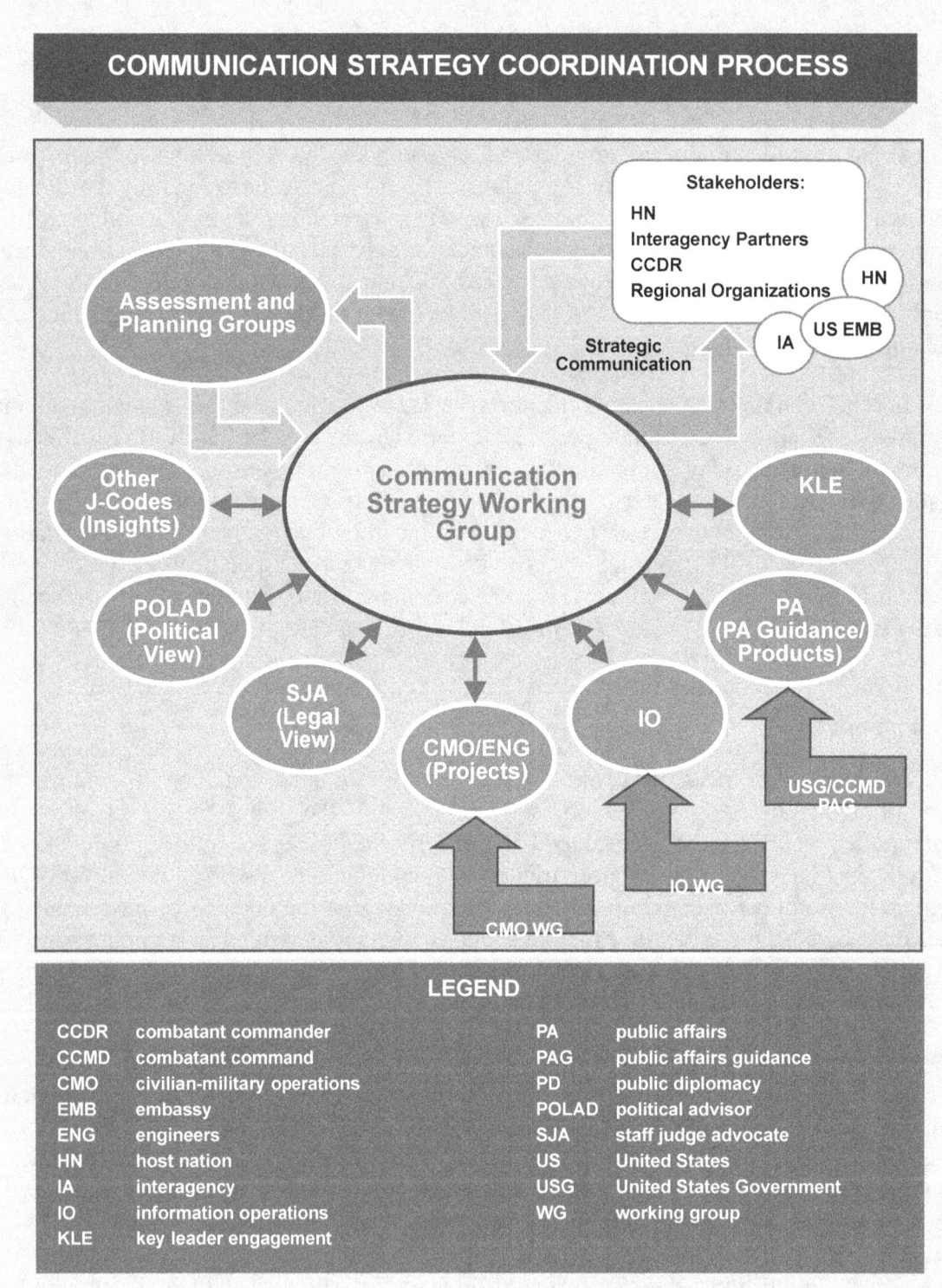

Figure A-1. Communications Strategy Coordination Process

3. Strategy Execution

PA plays a large role in the execution of the communications strategy through the dissemination of information and other traditional communication products to various audiences. Commanders also support strategy execution through key leader engagements with local leaders and civilians, and civil-military operation projects are planned to reinforce themes and messages. In addition, supporting the execution of the communications strategy in the competitive information environment requires the attention of everyone in the joint force, from the commander to the individual servicemember whose actions as well as words can be exploited by the adversary.

Intentionally Blank

APPENDIX B
ANNEX DEVELOPMENT

The guidance in this appendix relates to the development of annex F (Public Affairs) of the OPLAN format found in CJCSM 3122.03C, *Joint Operation Planning and Execution System (JOPES) Volume II, Planning Formats*.

1. **Situation**

    a. **General.** Assigns responsibilities and guidance for military PA actions (public information, command and internal information, and community engagement).

    b. **Enemy.** Identify expected actions of adversary forces and forces hostile to US interests.

    c. **Friendly.** Identify friendly agencies not under JFC control that will contribute to the PA effort. Include OASD(PA), DOS, US ambassadors, and multinational partners' PA programs, as appropriate.

    d. **Assumptions**

        (1) Describe HN preferences and/or sensitivities to be considered in developing and executing PA programs.

        (2) CCDRs should be prepared to host the DOD Media Pool during all stages of operations.

2. **Mission**

    State clearly and concisely the essential PA tasks to be accomplished as they relate to the overall operation.

3. **Execution**

    a. **Concept of Operations.** Outline PA efforts for the operation as part of JFC's mission and concept of the operation.

    b. **Tasks.** Outline the PA tasks to be completed during the above listed phases.

        (1) Provide any additional information to the supported CCDR and other supporting commands to include release authority and guidance on casualty and mortuary affairs, US and multinational prisoner of war (POW) or missing in action, and enemy prisoner of war (EPW) matters. Consider the establishment of a MOC. Outline PA VI and COMCAM requirements.

        (2) Provide detailed personnel and equipment support requirements to component commands. Address the following: access to the on-scene commander (OSC), supported CCDR, and the DOS representative, and to the secure voice circuit that connects the MOC;

access to hard copy message facilities between the same points; intertheater and intratheater transportation for escorted media; access to secure and nonsecure Internet access that connects the MOC to other PA outlets; access to digital imagery receiver equipment (could be through an intranet source); access to equipment for review and release of battle damage assessment-type video footage (could be through COMCAM). Coordinate this annex with logistics, communications, IO, and other planners to ensure required support is detailed.

(3) List Service, component command, and other supporting commands' support requirements.

c. **Coordinating Instructions.** Identify procedures for the following areas:

(1) Coordination of Release of Information. Provide detailed procedures for all supporting commands for handling or forwarding to the supported command queries, responses, and proposed news releases for clearance.

(2) PA Support to IO. Coordinate elements of PA with IO, as appropriate.

(3) Coordination of requests for interviews and news conferences with the individual's unit and Service PA offices for returned US personnel, and with the supporting staff judge advocate for EPW or detained personnel.

(4) Outline required PA coordination with other staff elements involved in release of information outside the command.

(5) Establish procedures for keeping PA historical records.

d. **Media Ground Rules**

(1) Release of Cleared Information. Establish means for release of information to be cleared and made available to the press.

(2) Categories of Releasable Information. Provide precise guidance for release of specific categories of information to the media.

(3) Categories of Information Not Releasable. Provide guidance on specific categories of information not releasable to the media.

4. Administration and Logistics

a. **Identify administration and logistics requirements for PA support.** Identify OPSEC procedures for PA personnel, include security review procedures. Identify procedures for providing PA, audio-visual, and VI coverage of the operation, including COMCAM requirements. Identify internal information requirements for subordinate and component commands.

b. **Identify detailed personnel and equipment support requirements.** Address the following:

(1) Secure voice and data connectivity between the MOC and OSC, supported commander, and the DOS representative.

(2) Intertheater and intratheater transportation for escorted media.

(3) Secure and nonsecure Internet between the MOC and other PA outlets.

(4) Digital imagery receiver equipment.

(5) Equipment for review and release of battle damage assessment-type video footage.

c. **MOC/Sub-MOC Support**

(1) **Personnel.** Identify required personnel.

(2) **Equipment.** Identify additional standard equipment required to allow MOC or sub-MOC operation in the operational area. Include tentage and individual field equipment on the same basis of issue as the accompanied unit.

(3) **Services.** Include basic food and shelter, water, office space and materials, clothing, transportation, etc., including portable copying machines, communications, automated data processing support, Internet and World Wide Web (www) access, and facsimile machines.

d. **Media/Media Pool Support.** Identify details on supporting the media to include: facilities, messing, billeting, force protection, immunizations, emergency medical treatment, transportation and communications, access to unclassified operational information, media pools, and other support.

(1) Outline plans for support of the media pool.

(a) Daily, comprehensive, unclassified operational briefings.

(b) Access to areas of ongoing operations.

(c) Access to key command and staff personnel.

(d) Designated officer from the supported command assigned to coordinate media pool requirements.

(e) Itinerary planning to enable media pool to disperse throughout the combat area to provide coverage of operations and to regroup periodically to share information and file stories.

(2) **Required Logistic Support.** Outline supported commander responsibilities for planning logistics support for pool and escort personnel. Support should address:

(a) Existing airlift to/from the point of origin and the operational area.

(b) Theater ground, sea, and air transportation available to the media.

(c) Messing, billeting, and reimbursement requirements.

(d) Issuance of any equipment considered appropriate to the situation (e.g., helmets, canteens, protective vest, and chemical protective gear).

(e) Access to communications facilities to file stories on an expedited basis.

(f) Medical support.

(g) Religious support.

5. **Command and Control**

Identify command relationships for PA including IOs cell participation (see Information Operations annex).

APPENDIX C
GUIDELINES FOR RELEASE OF INFORMATION

1. **Release of Information**

   a. **Release Authority and Public Statements**

   (1) Until release authority is delegated to them, units should forward queries and proposed news releases to the combatant command PAO.

   (2) No public statements concerning operations should be made by subordinate units without prior coordination with the combatant command PAO.

   b. **Assumptions**

   (1) All statements will be "on the record."

   (2) News media will have the ability to transmit instantaneous live reports from the operational area. Failure to plan for and accommodate the media will not stop them from reporting.

   (3) News media coverage will be highly competitive, with a tendency to seek access to the operational area and report events as they happen.

   (4) News media already on the scene may find ways to get to the operational area(s) and report the activities as they happen without regard for security concerns.

   (5) Independent media may be simultaneously deployed with the DOD Media Pool at the invitation of the Service component headquarters, under guidelines established by combatant command PAO that differ from those which apply to the DOD Media Pool.

   c. **Security Instructions**

   (1) PAOs submitting or staffing proposed products for public release must ensure that the information contained therein is fully coordinated and properly classified until approved for release.

   (2) Media are not usually given access to classified information that could jeopardize operations or endanger lives. In circumstances where this may be appropriate, PAOs must gain specific approval from the JFC.

   (3) Some members of the media may be briefed on planned operations prior to execution if they agree to withhold release until permitted to do so by the appropriate military authorities. Security of classified material is the responsibility of the information source ("security at the source") and is the normal method to ensure classified information is not compromised.

d. **Release below the JFC Level**

(1) Upon delegation of release authority, component and subordinate commanders may release information within the bounds of policy and guidance set forth by the joint force PAO or MOC director.

(2) A verbatim record of releases and news conferences should be maintained.

(3) Subordinate commanders should report the substance of any interview or responses to query to the MOC.

(4) News conferences should be videotaped or audiotaped.

e. **Department of Defense Directive 5400.07,** *Freedom of Information Act Program.* Requests for information under the Freedom of Information Act Program should be coordinated through the command's designated Freedom of Information Act representative or the servicing staff judge advocate or legal advisor if no such representative exists.

f. **Title 5, US Code, Section 552, The Privacy Act.** DOD personnel shall not disclose any personal information contained in any system of records except as authorized by DOD 5400.11-R, *DOD Privacy Program*, or other applicable law or regulation. Personnel willfully making such a disclosure when knowing that disclosure is prohibited are subject to possible criminal penalties and/or administrative sanctions.

2. **Discussions with the Media**

a. **Preparation.** Preparation results in more effective discussions with the media. Central to the process is identifying what information is to be released based on prevailing PAG and OPSEC. Commanders, briefers, and PA personnel should be aware of the basic facts of any operation and sensitive to the various consequences of communicating them to the public.

b. **Security.** "Security at the source" serves as the basis for ensuring that no information is released which jeopardizes OPSEC or the safety and privacy of joint military forces. Under this concept, individuals meeting with journalists are responsible for ensuring that no classified or sensitive information is revealed. This guidance also applies to photographers, who should be directed not to take pictures of classified areas or equipment or in any way to compromise sensitive information.

c. **Public Affairs Assessment.** Each operational situation will require a deliberate PA assessment in order to identify specific information to be released. The following categories of information are usually releasable, though individual situations may require modifications:

(1) The arrival of US units in the operational area once officially announced by DOD or by other commands in accordance with release authority granted by the OASD(PA). Information could include mode of travel (sea or air), date of departure, and home station or port.

(2) Approximate friendly force strength and equipment figures.

(3) Approximate friendly casualty and POW figures by Service. Approximate figures of adversary personnel detained during each action or operation.

(4) Nonsensitive, unclassified information regarding US air, land, sea, space, and special operations, past and present.

(5) In general terms, identification and location of military targets and objectives previously attacked and the types of ordnance expended.

(6) Date, time, or location of previous military missions and actions as well as mission results.

(7) Number of combat air patrol or reconnaissance missions and/or sorties flown in the operational area. Generic description of origin of air operations, such as "land" or "carrier-based."

(8) Weather and climate conditions.

(9) If appropriate, allied participation by type (ground units, ships, aircraft).

(10) Conventional operations' unclassified code names.

(11) Names of installations and assigned units.

(12) Size of friendly force participating in an action or operation using general terms such as "multi-battalion," or "naval task force."

(13) Types of forces involved (e.g., aircraft, ships, carrier strike groups, tank, and infantry units).

d. **Classified Information.** Classified aspects of equipment, procedures, and operations must be protected from disclosure to the media. In more general terms, information in the following categories of information should not be revealed because of potential jeopardy to future operations, the risk to human life, possible violation of HN and/or allied sensitivities, or the possible disclosure of intelligence methods and sources. While these guidelines serve to guide military personnel who talk with the media, they may also be used as ground rules for media coverage. The list is not necessarily complete and should be adapted to each operational situation.

(1) For US (or allied) units, specific numerical information on troop strength, aircraft, weapons systems, on-hand equipment, or supplies available for support of combat units. General terms should be used to describe units, equipment, and/or supplies.

(2) Any information that reveals details of future plans, operations, or strikes, including postponed or canceled operations.

(3) Information and imagery that would reveal the specific location of military forces or show the level of security at military installations or encampments. For datelines, stories will state that the report originates from general regions unless a specific country has acknowledged its participation.

(4) Rules of engagement.

(5) Information on intelligence activities, including sources and methods, lists of targets, and battle damage assessments.

(6) During an operation, specific information on friendly force troop movement or size, tactical deployments, and dispositions that would jeopardize OPSEC or lives. This would include unit designations and names of operations until released by the JFC.

(7) Identification of mission aircraft points of origin, other than as land- or carrier-based.

(8) Information on the effectiveness or ineffectiveness of weapon systems and tactics (to include, but not limited to adversary camouflage, cover, deception, targeting, direct and indirect fire, intelligence collection, or security measures).

(9) Specific identifying information on missing or downed personnel, aircraft, or sunken ships while search and rescue operations are planned or underway.

(10) SOFs' methods, equipment, or tactics which, if disclosed, would cause serious harm to the ability of these forces to accomplish their mission.

(11) Information on operational or support vulnerabilities that could be used against US or allied units until that information no longer provides tactical advantage to the adversary and is, therefore, released by the JFC. Damage and casualties may be described as "light," "moderate," or "heavy."

(12) Specific operating methods and tactics (e.g., offensive and defensive tactics or speed and formations). General terms such as "slow" or "fast" may be used.

(13) Requests for interviews or filming of EPWs or detained personnel must be coordinated through the staff judge advocate to ensure compliance with applicable laws and regulations including the law of war. Generally, photographing, filming, or other videotaping of EPWs or detained personnel for other than internal detention facility management purposes is likely to be prohibited. No individual in the custody or under the physical control of the USG, regardless of nationality or physical location, shall be subject to cruel, inhuman, or degrading treatment or punishment. Moreover, EPWs must at all times be protected against acts of violence or intimidation and against insults and public curiosity. Photos taken and used for nonofficial purposes may depict detainees in a degrading manner, thus violating international and US law.

APPENDIX D
SOURCES FOR DEFENSE MEDIA ACTIVITY

1. Defense Media Agency

The DMA is a consolidation of several DOD and Service media capabilties. Joint force PA staff may contact the DMA through www.dma.mil to request the following capabilities:

2. American Forces Radio and Television Service Assets

a. DOD 5120.20-R, *Management and Operation of American Forces Radio and Television Service,* outlines basic procedures to obtain AFRTS service. Contact the DMA for additional guidance and planning assistance.

b. The DMA can assist combatant command PA offices in planning and developing AFRTS systems to meet their contingency and CAP needs. Combatant command PA officials are responsible for planning for AFRTS in any operation as a joint command PA asset. The DMA encourage PA planners to involve the DMA in planning for exercise and during contingency operations. Extensive coordination may be required with other staff elements to coordinate communications frequency, power, and logistic requirements, based on the level of AFRTS support required for the operation.

c. AFRTS has several flexible response options available to support any operational requirement. Deployable equipment systems range from a small satellite receiver that can be connected to a TV in a common viewing area with an approximate weight of 100 pounds, through a staffed radio station with an approximate weight of 550 pounds and four personnel, to a staffed radio and TV network designed to cover an entire operational area. It should be noted that the small satellite receiver systems are being obtained by individual units to be deployed as unit equipment. AFIS and/or AFRTS encourages individual units to obtain these systems. A listing of units with these receiver systems can be obtained from AFIS and/or AFRTS.

3. Imagery

The DMA's DIMOC receives, processes, stores, and distributes classified and unclassified imagery products created by globally stationed and deployed DOD imagery producing personnel. PA officials can get customer service and request imagery through http://dodimagery.afis.osd.mil/index.html. The DIMOC also coordinates strategic VI requirements and plans with the DOD's operational forces. This includes assisting planners with VI plans (http://dodimagery.afis.osd.mil/about/dimoc.html).

4. Public Worldwide Web Operations

The DMA provides infrastructure for public-facing web pages for DOD customers. The DMA provides services necessary to create, sustain, maintain, and improve public-facing websites and their content.

5. Hometown News Program

The DMA provides hometown news program support to the DOD and military departments. PA staffs submit DD Form 2266, Hometown News Release Information. DMA develops and provides the American public (through over 10,000 subscribing commercial media outlets) news releases about individual members of the Services including AC and RC members, academy/Reserve Officer Training Corps cadets, and civil servants.

6. Afloat Media Systems Engineering and Maintenance Support

The DMA supports port-based support for shipboard direct-to-sailor TV receivers; the Shipboard Information, Training, and Entertainment System; shipboard distribution systems; and shipboard media department systems.

7. Blogger Engagement Services

The DMA facilitates DOD-wide PA operations by linking citizen journalists (bloggers) with DOD leaders. This includes telephone conferencing and transcription services.

8. Public Affairs and Visual Information Training

The DMA's DINFOS delivers PA, broadcasting, and VI training and education to initial, intermediate, and advanced-level DOD and interagency students (http://www.dinfos.dma.mil/).

9. Emerging Media Training, Education, and Testing

The DMA contributes to PA community proponency activities through the assessment, research, and testing of emerging media tools, techniques and technologies that may be of use within the DOD. This includes transfer of emerging media tools, techniques, and technologies to DOD components for practical application in PA operations.

APPENDIX E
JOINT PUBLIC AFFAIRS SUPPORT ELEMENT

1. **Overview**

a. The JPASE improves the ability of joint forces to operate successfully in today's complex information environment.

b. JPASE provides a trained, equipped, scalable, and expeditionary PA capability to include planning and media operations. JPASE is DOD's only joint PA unit and deploys globally to support JTF commanders' needs and provides scalable options that allow requesting combatant commands to tailor required capabilities.

c. JPASE provides PA training for JFCs and staffs through participation in major exercises, seminars, and planning events.

2. **Organization**

JPASE is organized to support the readiness demands of the global response force mission without sacrificing in the areas of training and proponency as shown in Figure E-1. The designation of global response force red, amber, or green relates to the degree of readiness of the team to deploy, with green being ready. This organization facilitates the integration of the JPASE reserves into operations and enhances command and control.

3. **Operational Support**

a. **Introduction.** JPASE serves as a standing joint PA capability for JFCs. JPASE can be rapidly deployed, in whole or in part, to support a variety of operational requirements through approved force request processes (e.g., RFF process).

(1) The deployment of all or part of JPASE provides the JFC with a standing mission-ready joint PA capability whenever and wherever needed. JPASE can respond to a CCDR's request for joint PA planning for potential contingencies, as well as for direct support of operations. As cohesive joint units, JPASE teams fit easily into force deployment packages but require logistical and life support from the requesting command.

(2) JPASE forces can be thought of as DOD "first responders" for joint PA. Like similar on-call forces, they are designed to respond quickly to the emergent situation until long-term forces are deployed.

b. **Capabilities.** Figure E-2 shows the joint PA competencies and capabilities that JPASE can provide to a JFC with scalable crisis response teams, as well as those capabilities JPASE can manage if augmented with additional forces, such as an Army mobile PA detachment and/or other Service capabilities. The size of the JPASE team and equipment required for support will depend upon the capabilities requested. Capabilities required are based on a PA mission analysis conducted by the appropriate combatant command PA staff in conjunction with JPASE leadership. Capabilities not organic to JPASE are noted in the far right column.

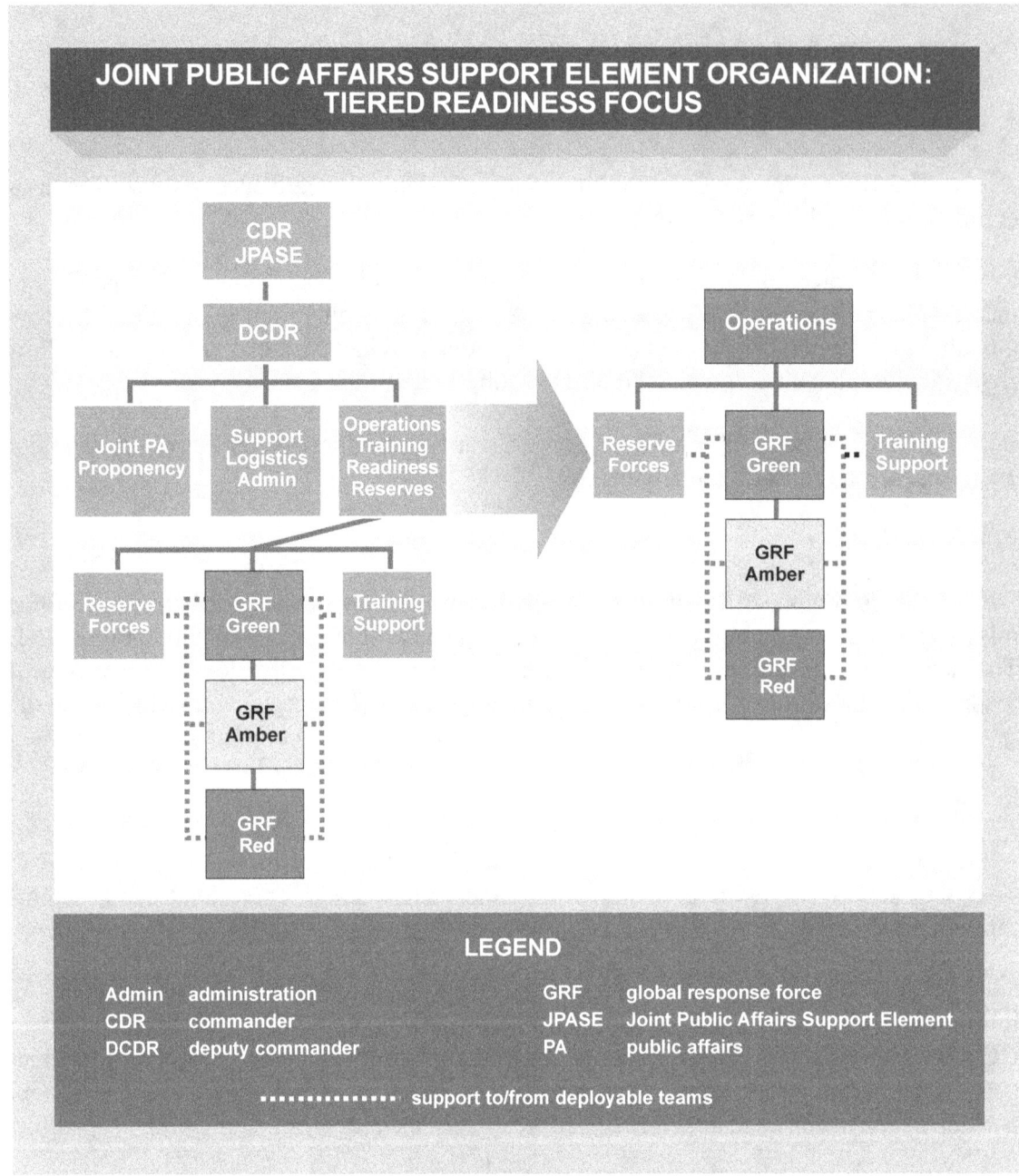

Figure E-1. Joint Public Affairs Support Element Organization: Tiered Readiness Focus

c. Deployment Considerations

(1) JPASE deploys upon approval by the Commander, United States Joint Forces Command (CDRUSJFCOM), as shown in Figure E-2. JPASE provides joint PA teams for emergent events or preplanned contingency operations. In the latter case, the requirement for JPASE capabilities should have been previously identified and coordinated between the supported CCDR and JPASE.

JOINT PUBLIC AFFAIRS CAPABILITIES			
Capability Area	Specific Capabilities	Organic	Support Needed
Advisor	Advise the commander on the requirements and employment of joint public affairs (PA) assets	X	
	Participate in strategic communication planning	X	
	Provide joint PA advice/counsel on the impact of proposed policy and operational decisions on public perception	X	
	Advise the commander on public impact of emerging events	X	
	Coordinate with higher and subordinate units on joint PA matters	X	
Planning and Operations	Participate in the boards, bureaus, centers, cells, and working group process	X	
	Direct joint PA operations in a joint operations area	X	
	Identify communication infrastructure requirements	X	
	Develop joint PA strategy	X	
	Develop/coordinate public affairs guidance (PAG) as necessary	X	
	Distribute PAG to subordinate units		X
	Summarize media coverage of operations	X	
	Coordinate with combat camera (COMCAM)/visual information (VI) assets	X	
	Conduct public information assessments (reach back)		X
Media Operations	Identify requirements for media support facilities/media operations centers (MOCs)	X	
	Coordinate establishment of necessary facilities/MOCs	X	
	Develop a media support plan	X	
	Conduct media accreditation	X	X
	Provide information to the media	X	
	Conduct/facilitate press briefings	X	
	Produce live uplink capability (Digital Video Information Distribution System)	X	
	Facilitate media embedding as appropriate	X	
	Coordinate with COMCAM/VI assets	X	
	Coordinate intratheater transportation for media.	X	
	Conduct media training for staff	X	
Publicly Accessible Websites	Coordinate content for established publicly accessible websites		X

JOINT PUBLIC AFFAIRS CAPABILITIES			
Capability Area	Specific Capabilities	Organic	Support Needed
Command Information	Manage/coordinate non-organic command information assets	X	
	Identify command internal information requirements		X
	Develop a command internal information plan		X
	Coordinate for a broadcast capability		X
	Produce command internal information products		X
Defense Support to Public Diplomacy	US embassy/consulate PA liaison	X	
	Other government agency coordination	X	
Visual Information	Develop a VI collection and dissemination plan	X	
	Coordinate VI acquisition requirements with COMCAM	X	
	Disseminate VI products *	X	
Community Engagement	Identify community engagement requirements		X
	Identify key publics and influencers		X
	Develop a community engagement plan		X
	Facilitate command interaction with local officials		X
* JPASE has limited imagery distribution capability			

Figure E-2. Joint Public Affairs Capabilities

(2) To ensure optimum availability of JPASE personnel for prescribed deployments, JPASE does not fill joint PA billets for which permanent party personnel are not assigned, provide individual augmentees to fill positions on joint manning documents, or participate in standard rotation of forces. Similarly, JPASE should not be requested unless combatant command and subordinate PA assets are fully engaged and unable to respond to the situation or are unable to provide the required capabilities. Figure E-3 depicts the deployment process as well as considerations for deployment.

d. **Size and Duration.** The capacity of JPASE to support deployments will vary based on personnel available and other operational requirements. JPASE typically maintains a ready team of eight personnel capable of responding to missions for a duration of 90-120 days. In the event that a deployment will exceed established JPASE limits, CCDRs are responsible for identifying requirements and fielding follow-on joint PA forces. If JPASE can support a deployment request, team members should be available on site 72 hours after notification (N+48).

e. **Requests for Joint Public Affairs Support Element**

(1) Commands request JPASE through approved force request processes in accordance with the USJFCOM joint enabling capability instructions. The CDRUSJFCOM has authority to approve JPASE deployments via a standing prepare to deploy order.

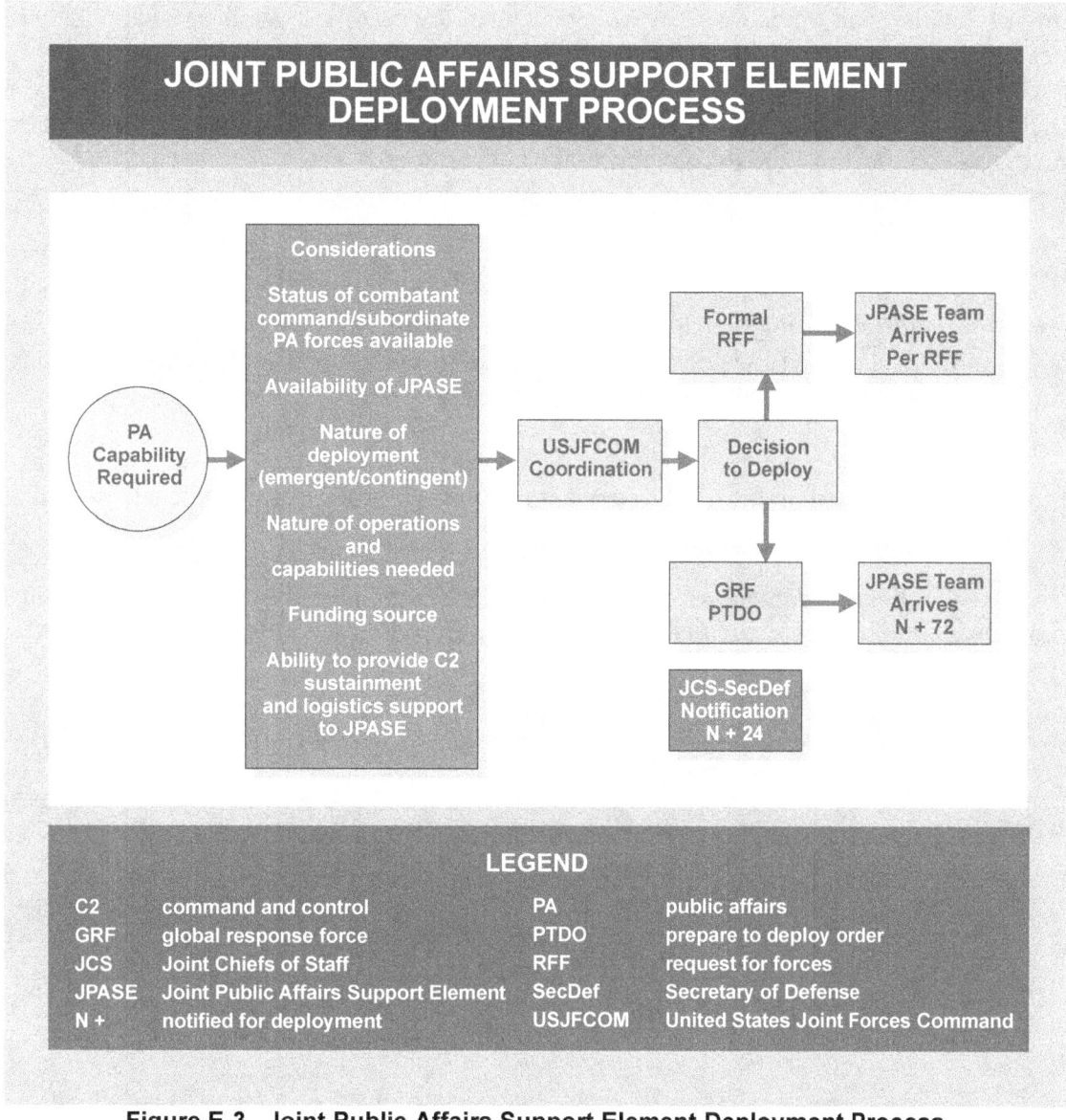

Figure E-3. Joint Public Affairs Support Element Deployment Process

Requests must identify specific joint PA capabilities required by the scope and breadth of the operation not the number of people.

(2) Past deployments demonstrate the need to get JPASE involved in force requirement discussions early to ensure that requesting commands know what capabilities JPASE has available at the time of the deployment and what capabilities would need to be sourced through other means. Informal coordination between the requesting command PAO and JPASE should be initiated at the earliest indication of a potential need. Once the required capabilities are identified, the requesting command PAO must formally identify the requirement for JPASE (and any other needed joint PA personnel) through the combatant command J-3.

f. **Operational Planning.** Early involvement of JPASE personnel in mission planning will help JFCs develop an integrated communications strategy that enhances and guides initial planning and operations. JPASE personnel are readily available to participate in operational planning (via teleconference or in person) for emergent events prior to deployment approval and the movement of the JPASE team into the operational area. Including JPASE in plan development will ensure the best use of follow-on JPASE team members and the best joint PA support to the commander.

g. **Required Support**

(1) **Communications Systems.** JPASE has very limited organic communications and information technology capability. Requesting commands must be prepared to provide, at a minimum, classified and unclassified connectivity, computers, and phones. Additional capabilities may be required based on the specific situation.

(2) **Logistics.** JPASE will require work spaces, billeting, messing, power, and transportation. Based on the need to move media from place to place, dedicated vehicular support may be required.

(3) **Force Protection.** JPASE personnel maintain ready inventory of personal protective equipment and are qualified with the 9mm pistol.

APPENDIX F
REFERENCES

The development of JP 3-61 is based upon the following primary references:

1. **Department of Defense Issuances**

    a. DODD 3600.01, *Information Operations (IO).*

    b. DODD 5105.74, *Defense Media Activity (DMA).*

    c. DODD 5120.20, *American Forces Radio and Television Service* (AFRTS).

    d. DODD 5122.05, *Assistant Secretary of Defense for Public Affairs (ASD[PA]).*

    e. DODD 5122.8, *Use of Military Carriers for Public Affairs Purposes.*

    f. DODD 5122.11, *Stars and Stripes Newspapers and Business Operations.*

    g. DODD 5230.09, *Clearance of DOD Information for Public Release.*

    h. DODD 5400.07, *DOD Freedom of Information Act (FOIA) Program.*

    i. DODD 5410.18, *Public Affairs Community Relations Policy.*

    j. DODI 5040.04, *Joint Combat Camera (COMCAM) Program.*

    k. DODI 5200.01, *DOD Information Security Program and Protection of Sensitive Compartmented Information.*

    l. DODI 5230.29, *Security and Policy Review of DOD Information for Public Release.*

    m. DODI 5400.13, *Public Affairs Operations.*

    n. DODI 5400.14, *Procedures for Joint Public Affairs Operations.*

    o. DODI 5405.3, *Development of Proposed Public Affairs Guidance (PPAG).*

    p. DODI 5410.19, *Public Affairs Community Relations Policy Implementation.*

    q. DODI 5435.2, *Delegation of Authority to Approve Travel In and Use of Military Carriers for Public Affairs Purposes.*

    r. DOD 4515.13-R, *Air Transportation Eligibility.*

    s. DOD 5120.20-R, *Management and Operation of American Forces Radio and Television Service (AFRTS).*

t. Directive-Type Memorandum (DTM) 09-026, *Responsible and Effective Use of Internet-based Capabilities.*

u. *Joint Travel Regulations, Volume II, Department of Defense Civilian Personnel.*

v. *Quadrennial Defense Review Report 2010.*

2. **Chairman of the Joint Chiefs of Staff Issuances**

a. CJCSI 1301.01C, *Individual Augmentation Procedures.*

b. CJCSI 3205.01B, *Joint Combat Camera.*

c. CJCSI 3210.01B, *Joint Information Operations Policy.*

d. CJCSI 3213.01C, *Joint Operations Security.*

e. CJCSM 3122.03C, *Joint Operation Planning and Execution System, Volume I, Planning Formats.*

3. **Joint Publications**

a. JP 1, *Doctrine for the Armed Forces of the United States.*

b. JP 1-02, *Department of Defense Dictionary of Military and Associated Terms.*

c. JP 2-0, *Joint Intelligence.*

d. JP 2-01, *Joint and National Intelligence Support to Military Operations.*

e. JP 2-01.3, *Joint Intelligence Preparation of the Operational Environment.*

f. JP 3-0, *Joint Operations.*

g. JP 3-07.2, *Antiterrorism.*

h. JP 3-07.3, *Peace Operations.*

i. JP 3-07.4, *Joint Counterdrug Operations.*

j. JP 3-13, *Information Operations.*

k. JP 3-13.2, *Military Information Support Operations.*

l. JP 3-13.3, *Operations Security.*

m. JP 3-13.4, *Military Deception.*

n. JP 3-14, *Space Operations.*

o. JP 3-27, *Homeland Defense*.

p. JP 3-28, *Civil Support.*

q. JP 3-29, *Foreign Humanitarian Assistance.*

r. JP 3-57, *Civil-Military Operations.*

s. JP 3-68, *Noncombatant Evacuation Operations.*

t. JP 6-0, *Joint Communications System.*

4. **Multi-Service Publication**

FM 3-55.12/MCRP 3-33.7A/NTTP 3-13.12/AFTTP 3-2.41, *Multi-Service Tactics, Techniques, and Procedures for Combat Camera Operations.*

Intentionally Blank

APPENDIX G
ADMINISTRATIVE INSTRUCTIONS

1. User Comments

Users in the field are highly encouraged to submit comments on this publication to: Commander, United States Joint Forces Command, Joint Warfighting Center, ATTN: Doctrine and Education Group, 116 Lake View Parkway, Suffolk, VA 23435-2697. These comments should address content (accuracy, usefulness, consistency, and organization), writing, and appearance.

2. Authorship

The lead agent for this publication is the United States Joint Forces Command, Public Affairs. The Joint Staff doctrine sponsor for this publication is the Joint Staff, Public Affairs.

3. Supersession

This publication supersedes JP 3-61, 9 May 2005, *Public Affairs.*

4. Change Recommendations

a. Recommendations for urgent changes to this publication should be submitted:

TO: CDRUSJFCOM NORFOLK VA//JO1P//
INFO: JOINT STAFF WASHINGTON DC//J7-JEDD//
   CDRUSJFCOM SUFFOLK VA//DEG//

b. Routine changes should be submitted electronically to the Commander, Joint Warfighting Center, Doctrine and Education Group, and info the Director for Operational Plans and Joint Force Development (J-7)/Joint Education and Doctrine Division (JEDD), via the CJCS Joint Electronic Library (JEL) at http://www.dtic.mil/doctrine.

c. When a Joint Staff directorate submits a proposal to the CJCS that would change source document information reflected in this publication, that directorate will include a proposed change to this publication as an enclosure to its proposal. The Military Services and other organizations are requested to notify the Joint Staff/J-7, when changes to source documents reflected in this publication are initiated.

d. Record of Changes:

CHANGE NUMBER	COPY NUMBER	DATE OF CHANGE	DATE ENTERED	POSTED BY	REMARKS

5. Distribution of Publications

a. Local reproduction is authorized and access to unclassified publications is unrestricted. However, access to and reproduction authorization for classified joint publications must be in accordance with DOD 5200.1-R, *Information Security Program*.

b. The Joint Staff J-7 will not print copies of JPs for distribution. Electronic versions are available on JDEIS at https://jdeis.js.mil (NIPRNET), or https://jdeis.js.smil.mil (SIPRNET) and on the JEL at http://www.dtic.mil/doctrine (NIPRNET).

c. Only approved joint publications and joint test publications are releasable outside the combatant commands, Services, and Joint Staff. Release of any classified joint publication to foreign governments or foreign nationals must be requested through the local embassy (Defense Attaché Office) to DIA, Defense Foreign Liaison/IE-3, 200 MacDill Blvd., Bolling AFB, Washington, DC 20340-5100.

d. CD-ROM. Upon request of a JDDC member, the Joint Staff J-7 will produce and deliver one CD-ROM with current JPs.

GLOSSARY
PART I—ABBREVIATIONS AND ACRONYMS

AC	Active Component
AFIS	American Forces Information Service
AFRTS	American Forces Radio and Television Service
AFTTP	Air Force tactics, techniques, and procedures
ASD(PA)	Assistant Secretary of Defense (Public Affairs)
CA	civil affairs
CAISE	civil authority information support element
CAP	crisis action planning
CBRN CM	chemical, biological, radiological, and nuclear consequence management
CCDR	combatant commander
CD	counterdrug
CDRUSJFCOM	Commander, United States Joint Forces Command
CJCS	Chairman of the Joint Chiefs of Staff
CJCSI	Chairman of the Joint Chiefs of Staff instruction
CJCSM	Chairman of the Joint Chiefs of Staff manual
CMO	civil-military operations
CMOC	civil-military operations center
CNO	computer network operations
COA	course of action
COM	chief of mission
COMCAM	combat camera
CONOPS	concept of operations
CS	civil support
CWMD	combating weapons of mass destruction
DCE	defense coordinating element
DCO	defense coordinating officer
DHS	Department of Homeland Security
DIMOC	Defense Imagery Management Operations Center
DINFOS	Defense Information School
DMA	Defense Media Activity
DOD	Department of Defense
DODD	Department of Defense directive
DODI	Department of Defense instruction
DOS	Department of State
DSCA	defense support of civil authorities
DSPD	defense support to public diplomacy
EPW	enemy prisoner of war
ESF	emergency support function

EW	electronic warfare
EXORD	execute order
FEMA	Federal Emergency Management Agency
FHA	foreign humanitarian assistance
FM	field manual (Army)
HN	host nation
IAW	in accordance with
ICEPP	Incident Communications Emergency Policy and Procedures
IGO	intergovernmental organization
INFOSEC	information security
IO	information operations
J-2	intelligence directorate of a joint staff
J-3	operations directorate of a joint staff
JFC	joint force commander
JIC	joint information center
JIPOE	joint intelligence preparation of the operational environment
JOA	joint operations area
JOPP	joint operation planning process
JP	joint publication
JPASE	Joint Public Affairs Support Element
JSOTF	joint special operations task force
JTF	joint task force
MCRP	Marine Corps reference publication
MILDEC	military deception
MISO	military information support operations
MOC	media operations center
NEO	noncombatant evacuation operation
NGO	nongovernmental organization
NICCL	National Incident Communications Conference Line
NRF	National Response Framework
NTTP	Navy tactics, techniques, and procedures
OASD(PA)	Office of the Assistant Secretary of Defense (Public Affairs)
OGA	other government agency
OPLAN	operation plan

OPORD   operation order
OPSEC   operations security
OSC   on-scene commander

PA   public affairs
PAG   public affairs guidance
PAO   public affairs officer
PD   public diplomacy
PIO   public information officer
PO   peace operations
POW   prisoner of war
PPAG   proposed public affairs guidance

RC   Reserve Component
RFF   request for forces

SC   strategic communication
SecDef   Secretary of Defense
SOF   special operations forces

TV   television

USG   United States Government
USJFCOM   United States Joint Forces Command

VI   visual information

WMD   weapons of mass destruction

American Forces Radio and Television Service. A worldwide radio and television broadcasting organization that provides United States military commanders overseas and at sea with sufficient electronic media resources to effectively communicate theater, local, Department of Defense, and Service-unique command information to their personnel and family members. Also called **AFRTS.** (Approved for replacement of "Armed Forces Radio and Television Service" in JP 1-02.)

civil affairs. Designated Active and Reserve Component forces and units organized, trained, and equipped specifically to conduct civil affairs operations and to support civil-military operations. Also called **CA.** (JP 1-02. SOURCE: JP 3-57)

civil-military operations. The activities of a commander that establish, maintain, influence, or exploit relations between military forces, governmental and nongovernmental civilian organizations and authorities, and the civilian populace in a friendly, neutral, or hostile operational area in order to facilitate military operations, to consolidate and achieve operational US objectives. Civil-military operations may include performance by military forces of activities and functions normally the responsibility of the local, regional, or national government. These activities may occur prior to, during, or subsequent to other military actions. They may also occur, if directed, in the absence of other military operations. Civil-military operations may be performed by designated civil affairs, by other military forces, or by a combination of civil affairs and other forces. Also called **CMO.** (JP 1-02. SOURCE: JP 3-57)

civil-military operations center. An organization normally composed of civil affairs, established to plan and facilitate coordination of activities of the Armed Forces of the United States with indigenous populations and institutions, the private sector, intergovernmental organizations, nongovernmental organizations, multinational forces, and other governmental agencies in support of the joint force commander. Also called **CMOC.** (JP 1-02. SOURCE: JP 3-57)

combat camera. The acquisition and utilization of still and motion imagery in support of operational and planning requirements across the range of military operations and during joint exercises. Also called **COMCAM.** (Approved for incorporation into JP 1-02.)

combat visual information support center. None. (Approved for removal from JP 1-02.)

command information. Communication by a military organization directed to the internal audience that creates an awareness of the organization's goals, informs them of significant developments affecting them and the organization, increases their effectiveness as ambassadors of the organization, and keeps them informed about what is going on in the organization. Also called **internal information.** (Approved for incorporation into JP 1-02.)

community engagement. Those public affairs activities that support the relationship between military and civilian communities. (Approved for inclusion in JP 1-02.)

community relations. None. (Approved for removal from JP 1-02.)

community relations program. None. (Approved for removal from JP 1-02.)

country team. The senior, in-country, US coordinating and supervising body, headed by the chief of the US diplomatic mission, and composed of the senior member of each represented US department or agency, as desired by the chief of the US diplomatic mission. Also called **CT**. (JP 1-02. SOURCE: JP 3-07.4)

external audience. All people who are not US military members, Department of Defense civilian employees, and their immediate families. (Approved for incorporation into JP 1-02.)

host nation. A nation which receives the forces and/or supplies of allied nations, and/or NATO organizations to be located on, to operate in, or to transit through its territory. Also called **HN**. (JP 1-02. SOURCE: JP 3-57)

internal audience. US military members and Department of Defense civilian employees and their immediate families. (Approved for incorporation into JP 1-02.)

joint information bureau. None. (Approved for removal from JP 1-02.)

Joint Public Affairs Support Element. A deployable unit assigned to assist a joint force commander in developing and training public affairs forces in joint, interagency, and multinational environments. Also called **JPASE.** (Approved for inclusion in JP 1-02.)

media operations center. A facility established by the joint force commander to serve as the focal point for the interface between the military and the media during the conduct of joint operations. Also called **MOC.** (Approved for inclusion in JP 1-02.)

media pool. A limited number of news media who represent a larger number of news media organizations for purposes of news gathering and sharing of material during a specified activity. Pooling is typically used when news media support resources cannot accommodate a large number of journalists. (JP 1-02. SOURCE: JP 3-61)

message. 1. Any thought or idea expressed briefly in a plain or secret language and prepared in a form suitable for transmission by any means of communication. (JP 6-0) 2. A narrowly focused communication directed at a specific audience to support a specific theme. (Approved for incorporation into JP 1-02 with JP 6-0 as the source JP for Definition #1.)

military journalist. A US Service member or Department of Defense civilian employee providing photographic, print, radio, or television command information for military internal audiences. (JP 1-02. SOURCE: JP 3-61)

news media representative. An individual employed by a civilian radio or television station, newspaper, newsmagazine, periodical, or news agency to gather and report on a newsworthy event. Also called **NMR.** (JP 1-02. SOURCE: JP 3-61)

official information. Information that is owned by, produced for or by, or is subject to the control of the United States Government. (Approved for incorporation into JP 1-02 with JP 3-61 as the source JP.)

operations security. A process of identifying critical information and subsequently analyzing friendly actions attendant to military operations and other activities to: a. identify those actions that can be observed by adversary intelligence systems; b. determine indicators that adversary intelligence systems might obtain that could be interpreted or pieced together to derive critical information in time to be useful to adversaries; and c. select and execute measures that eliminate or reduce to an acceptable level the vulnerabilities of friendly actions to adversary exploitation. Also called **OPSEC.** (JP 1-02. SOURCE: JP 3-13.3)

public affairs. Those public information, command information, and community engagement activities directed toward both the external and internal publics with interest in the Department of Defense. Also called **PA.** (Approved for incorporation into JP 1-02.)

public affairs assessment. An analysis of the news media and public environments to evaluate the degree of understanding about strategic and operational objectives and military activities and to identify levels of public support. It includes judgment about the public affairs impact of pending decisions and recommendations about the structure of public affairs support for the assigned mission. (JP 1-02. SOURCE: JP 3-61)

public affairs ground rules. None. (Approved for removal from JP 1-02.)

public affairs guidance. Constraints and restraints established by proper authority regarding public information, command information, and community relations activities. It may also address the method(s), timing, location, and other details governing the release of information to the public. Also called **PAG.** (Approved for incorporation into JP 1-02.)

public diplomacy. 1. Those overt international public information activities of the United States Government designed to promote United States foreign policy objectives by seeking to understand, inform, and influence foreign audiences and opinion makers, and by broadening the dialogue between American citizens and institutions and their counterparts abroad. 2. In peace building, civilian agency efforts to promote an understanding of the reconstruction efforts, rule of law, and civic responsibility through public affairs and international public diplomacy operations. Its objective is to promote and sustain consent for peace building both within the host nation and externally in the region and in the larger international community. (JP 1-02. SOURCE: JP 3-07.3)

public information. Within public affairs, that information of a military nature, the dissemination of which is consistent with security and approved for release. (Approved for incorporation into JP 1-02.)

security review. The process of reviewing information and products prior to public release to ensure the material will not jeopardize ongoing or future operations. (Approved for incorporation into JP 1-02.)

strategic communication. Focused United States Government efforts to understand and engage key audiences to create, strengthen, or preserve conditions favorable for the advancement of United States Government interests, policies, and objectives through the use of coordinated programs, plans, themes, messages, and products synchronized with the actions of all instruments of national power. Also called **SC**. (JP 1-02. SOURCE: JP 5-0)

visual information. Various visual media with or without sound. Generally, visual information includes still and motion photography, audio video recording, graphic arts, visual aids, models, display, visual presentations. Also called **VI**. (Approved for incorporation into JP 1-02.)

visual information documentation. None. (Approved for removal from JP 1-02.)

Intentionally Blank

JOINT DOCTRINE PUBLICATIONS HIERARCHY

JP 1
JOINT DOCTRINE
JP 1-0
PERSONNEL
JP 2-0
INTELLIGENCE
JP 3-0
OPERATIONS
JP 4-0
LOGISTICS
JP 5-0
PLANS
JP 6-0
COMMUNICATIONS SYSTEM

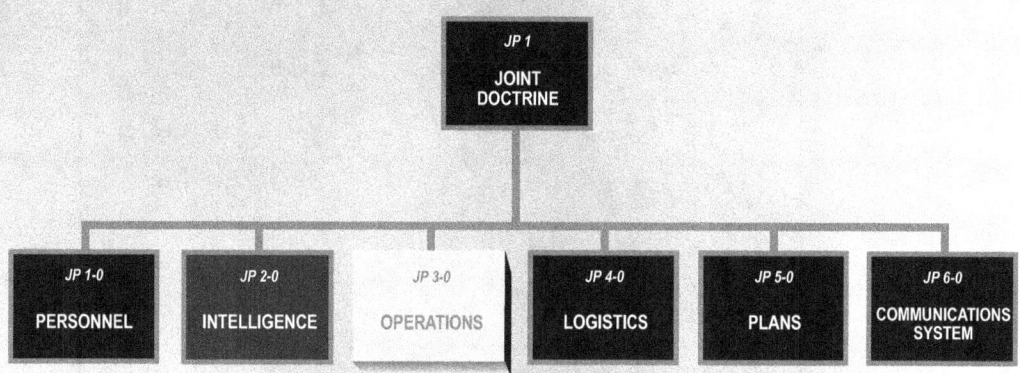

All joint publications are organized into a comprehensive hierarchy as shown in the chart above. **Joint Publication (JP) 3-61** is in the **Operations** series of joint doctrine publications. The diagram below illustrates an overview of the development process:

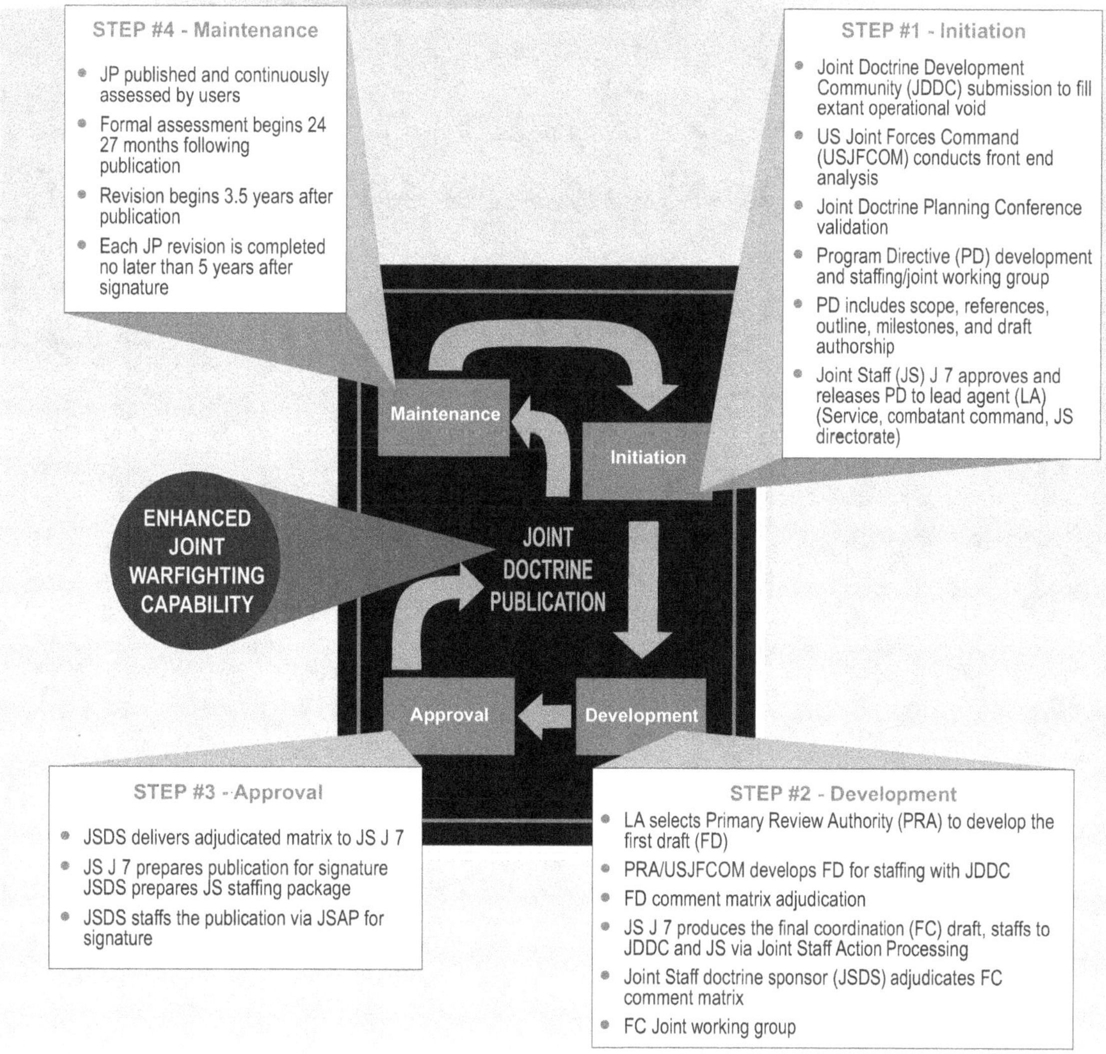

STEP #4 - Maintenance
JP published and continuously assessed by users
Formal assessment begins 24 27 months following publication
Revision begins 3.5 years after publication
Each JP revision is completed no later than 5 years after signature
STEP #1 - Initiation
Joint Doctrine Development Community (JDDC) submission to fill extant operational void
US Joint Forces Command (USJFCOM) conducts front end analysis
Joint Doctrine Planning Conference validation
Program Directive (PD) development and staffing/joint working group
PD includes scope, references, outline, milestones, and draft authorship
Joint Staff (JS) J 7 approves and releases PD to lead agent (LA) (Service, combatant command, JS directorate)
Maintenance
Initiation
ENHANCED JOINT WARFIGHTING CAPABILITY
JOINT DOCTRINE PUBLICATION
Approval
Development
STEP #3 - Approval
JSDS delivers adjudicated matrix to JS J 7
JS J 7 prepares publication for signature JSDS prepares JS staffing package
JSDS staffs the publication via JSAP for signature
STEP #2 - Development
LA selects Primary Review Authority (PRA) to develop the first draft (FD)
PRA/USJFCOM develops FD for staffing with JDDC
FD comment matrix adjudication
JS J 7 produces the final coordination (FC) draft, staffs to JDDC and JS via Joint Staff Action Processing
Joint Staff doctrine sponsor (JSDS) adjudicates FC comment matrix
FC Joint working group